The Unofficial United Methodist Handbook

Have Horse, Will Travel

The early leaders and shapers of United Methodism did their extensive traveling by horse or by foot. Thousands and thousands of miles. Surely, God gives those horses some of the credit for the spread of the gospel—it wouldn't be the first time that God used some unsuspecting agent to bring grace! "Saint Blaze" or "Saint Saddle" has a nice ring to it.

Often those circuit-riding preachers are pictured riding sedately, reading important books. That's a good image, helpful for understanding the care they gave to thought and discipline and truth and scholarship and all those other nice things. But surely sometimes the sheer excitement of the mission gave both horse and rider a burst of enthusiastic energy. Surely there was a mix of quiet reflection and bubbling joy, even laughter. Surely sometimes things got just a bit out of hand.

That's what's happening with this cover icon. Is it John Wesley? Is it Philip William Otterbein? Is it you, loyal reader? Whoever it is, it is time to get with the plan: ready to ride with laughter and tears and a love of God! Giddyap!

Unofficial
The United Methodist Handbook
^

Abingdon Press
Nashville

THE UNOFFICIAL UNITED METHODIST HANDBOOK

Part of this book was originally published as *The Lutheran Handbook* © 2005 Augsburg Fortress and *The Christian Handbook* © 2005 Augsburg Fortress.

Copyright © 2007 by Abingdon Press

LIBRARY OF CONGRESS CATALOGING-IN-PUBLICATION DATA

The unofficial United Methodist handbook / [content editor, F. Belton Joyner].
    p. cm.
  Includes bibliographical references and index.
  ISBN 978-0-687-64185-7 (binding: pbk.,adhesive perfect : alk. paper)
  1. United Methodist Church (U.S.)--Handbooks, manuals, etc.   I. Joyner, F. Belton.

BX8382.2.U56 2007
287'.6--dc22
                                    2007001176

Scripture quotations are from the New Revised Standard Version Bible, copyright © 1989, Division of Christian Education of the National Council of the Churches of Christ in the United States of America.

Page 64: Martin Boehm quotation from *The History of the Evangelical United Brethren Church* by J. Bruce Behney and Paul H. Eller, © 1979, Abingdon Press, page 62.

Pages 83–91: Sources for the charts include reference materials from *Information Please*,® New York Times Public Library/Hyperion, Rose Publishing, Time-Life, and Wadsworth Group/Thomas Learning.

Page 217: Information for this chart appeared in *John Wesley's Message Today* by Lovett H. Weems Jr., © 1982 Discipleship Resources; 1991 Abingdon Press.

Content editor: F. Belton Joyner Jr.
Cover design: Rick Schroeppel
Interior illustrations: Brenda Brown

Contributing writers: F. Belton Joyner Jr., Suzanne Burke, Lou Carlozo, Giacomo Cassese, Mark Gardner, Wes Halula, Sarah Henrich, Mark Hinton, Sue Houglum, Rolf Jacobson, Susan M. Lang, Andrea Lee, Daniel Levitin, Terry Marks, Catherine Malotky, Jeffrey S. Nelson, Rebecca Ninke, Eliseo Pérez-Álvarez, Dawn Rundman, Jonathan Rundman, Ted Schroeder, Ken Sundet Jones, Hans Wiersma

07 08 09 10 11 12 13 14 15 16—10 9 8 7 6 5 4 3 2 1

MANUFACTURED IN THE UNITED STATES OF AMERICA

CONTENTS

Everyday Stuff

Bible Stuff

This Book Belongs To

Name _____

Address _____

_____

E-mail _____

Telephone _____

If this book is found, please read it and then either call me (at your expense) or return it to me in a plain, brown, unmarked envelope. You can buy your own copy at a nearby Cokesbury Bookstore.

Birth date _____

Baptismal birth date _____

Profession of faith date _____

Churches I've belonged to:*   *Years of membership*

_____   _____

_____   _____

_____   _____

_____   _____

_____   _____

_____   _____

_____   _____

   **If a particularly juicy scandal is involved in your departure, please provide full details for the benefit of future church historians.*

About My Congregation

Name _____

Address _____

_____

Year organized/founded _____

My pastor(s) _____

_____

_____

_____

Number of baptized members* _____

Number of professing members* _____

Average weekly worship attendance _____

Facts about my denomination _____

_____

_____

Other information about my congregation and faith

_____

_____

_____

*In The United Methodist Church, baptized persons are consid-
ered full members of the local church, the denomination, and the
church universal; only those baptized persons who have made pro-
fessions of faith are counted for church membership statistical
purposes or are eligible for church office.

PREFACE

Please Be Advised:

Lots of books, pamphlets, and booklets have been written through the centuries as companions for average folks who wanted help navigating their way through a complicated subject. *The Boy Scout Handbook* comes to mind, for example. So do *The American Red Cross First Aid and Safety Handbook*, *Tune and Repair Your Own Piano: A Practical and Theoretical Guide to the Tuning of All Keyboard Stringed Instruments*, and *National Audubon Society's Field Guide to North American Reptiles and Amphibians*. They stand as testimony to the average person's need for a guide to both the vast truths and complex detail that make up a particular area of interest. These books turn complicated, inaccessible ideas into simple, easy-to-understand concepts, and, if necessary, into action steps that are easy to follow.

Likewise, *The Unofficial United Methodist Handbook* follows this format. Here, you will discover a combination of reliable, historical, and theological information alongside some fun facts and very useful tips on being a churchgoing follower of Jesus Christ, all presented in that practical United Methodist, down-to-earth, tongue-in-cheek sort of way. After all, John Wesley, one of our founders, referred to all of this stuff as "practical divinity."

You will also discover that this book is intended for learning and enjoyment. (Some Christians have trouble doing the latter until they've first suffered through the former.) It's meant to spur conversation, to inform and edify, and to make you laugh. Think of the book as a comedian with a dry sense of humor and a degree in theology. It can be used in the classroom with students or at the dinner table with family or in solitude. You might want to take care not to read the book in public places where out loud giggling and occasional guffawing is frowned upon.

But however you use it, use it! We've cut the corners off so you can throw it in your backpack or stuff it in a pocket. It's printed on paper that accepts either ink or pencil nicely, so feel free to write and highlight in it (and there's room for notes in the back). The cover is this fancy, nearly indestructible stuff that will last forever too, so don't worry about spilling soda pop or coffee on it. We've even heard it can sustain a direct hit from a nuclear missile. You will, of course, want to keep it forever in your possession; if you threw it away, it would take a gadzillion years to disintegrate in a public landfill.

Anyway, the point is this: being a follower of Jesus is hard enough without having to navigate the faith journey—let alone the maze of church culture—all alone. Sooner or later everyone needs a companion.

CHURCH STUFF

Every well-prepared United Methodist should have a basic understanding of United Methodist teachings and where they came from.

Plus, since every church goes about worship in a slightly different way, it might take a little time to get the hang of things—especially if you're new to a congregation.

This section includes:

- Essential facts about the United Methodist brand of the Christian faith. (If you already know most of these things, congratulate the person who sits in the pew to the left of the person on your right.)
- Practical advice for singing hymns, taking Communion, and getting to know the people in your congregation.
- Hints for enjoying worship—even when you're having a bad day.

HOW TO GET TO
KNOW YOUR PASTOR

Pastors (or preacher or reverend or brother or sister or padre
or hey, you or whatever you call this person in your part of
the country) play an important role in the daily life of your
congregation and the community. Despite their churchly
profession, fancy robes, and knowledge of Greek, pastors
experience the same kinds of ups and downs as everyone
else. They value member efforts to meet, connect with, and
support them.

❶ Connect with your pastor after worship.
After the worship service, join others in line to shake the
pastor's hand. Sharing a comment about the sermon,
readings, or hymns lets the pastor know that his or her
worship planning time is appreciated. If your congregation doesn't practice the dismissal line, find other ways
to make that personal connection.

**❷ Pray daily for your pastor, because he or she doesn't
just work on Sunday.**
Your pastor has many responsibilities, like visiting
members in the hospital, writing sermons, and figuring
out who can help drain the flooded church basement.
In your prayers, ask God to grant your pastor health,
strength, and wisdom to face the many challenges of
leading a congregation.

**❸ Ask your pastor to share with you why he or she
entered this form of ministry.**
There are many reasons why a pastor may have enrolled
in seminary to become an ordained or licensed minister.
Be prepared for a story that may surprise you.

❹ Stop by your pastor's office to talk, or consider making an appointment to get to know him or her. Pastors welcome the opportunity to connect with church members at times other than worship. As you would with any drop-in visit, be sensitive to the fact that your pastor may be quite busy. A scheduled appointment just to chat could provide a welcome break in your pastor's day. How about offering to drive the pastor to an out-of-town ball game? Or to go as your guest to The Pink Pickle (or whatever the new restaurant is called)?

Getting to know your pastor can help you get more out of church and can help you give more of yourself through the church.

HOW TO SURVIVE FOR ONE HOUR IN AN UN-AIR-CONDITIONED CHURCH

Getting trapped in an overheated sanctuary is a common churchgoing experience. The key is to minimize your heat gain and electrolyte loss.

1 Plan ahead.
When possible, scout out the sanctuary ahead of time to locate optimal seating near fans or open windows. Consider where the sun will be during the worship service and avoid sitting under direct sunlight. Bring a bottle of water for each person in your group. It is considered bad form to smirk at those who get trapped in the hot spots while you, ignoring Christian charity, have taken the cool corners for yourself.

2 Maintain your distance from others.
Human beings disperse heat and moisture as a means of cooling themselves. An average-size person puts off about as much heat as a 75-watt lightbulb. The front row will likely be empty and available.

Use your bulletin as a personal fan to keep cool.

3 Remain still.
Fidgeting will only make your heat index rise.

④ Think cool thoughts.
Your mental state can affect your physical disposition. If the heat distracts you from worship, imagine you're sitting on a big block of ice.

⑤ Dress for survival.
Wear only cool, breathable fabrics.

⑥ Avoid acolyte or choir robes when possible.
Formal robes are especially uncomfortable in the heat. If you must wear one, make sure to wear lightweight clothes underneath.

⑦ Pray.
Jesus survived on prayer in the desert for 40 days. Lifting and extending your arms in an open prayer position may help cool your body by dispersing excess heat. Choose the moment in the worship most conducive to lifting your arms; otherwise, others may wonder why you continue to signal a touchdown in the middle of the service.

On hot days, wear light clothing underneath acolyte or choir robes.

Be Aware

- Carry a personal fan—or use your bulletin as a substitute.
- Worship services scheduled for one hour sometimes will run long. Plan ahead.

HOW TO RESPOND WHEN SOMEONE SITS IN YOUR PEW

There are certain situations in which we invite visitors into our little sphere of experience—like at church. These situations need not be cause for alarm.

1 Smile and greet the "intruders."
Oftentimes they are visitors to your congregation. Make solid eye contact so they know you mean it, shake hands with them, and leave no impression that they've done something wrong.

2 View the "intrusion" as an opportunity.
Remember, you don't own the pew; you just borrow it once a week. Take the opportunity to get out of your rut and sit someplace new. This will physically emphasize a change in your perspective and may yield new spiritual discoveries.

3 If you can tell that your new friends feel uncomfortable at having displaced you, despite your efforts to the contrary, make an extra effort to welcome them.
Consider taking them to brunch after church to become acquainted. If there are too many for you to foot the bill, consider inviting them to accompany you on a "go Dutch" basis.

4 If Christian hospitality is not in your arsenal of virtues, consider standing at the end of the pew, locking your crossed arms, as you look exasperated and sigh deeply.
Explain to onlookers that if you do not sit in that pew, God might not be able to find you.

HOW TO USE A WORSHIP BULLETIN

Many United Methodist congregations offer a printed resource called a bulletin to assist worshipers. The bulletin may contain the order of the service, liturgical information, music listings, the day's Bible readings, and important community announcements.

1 Arrive early.
A few extra minutes before worship will allow you to scan the bulletin and prepare for the service.

2 Receive the bulletin from the usher.
Upon entering the worship space, an usher will give you a bulletin. Some congregations stack bulletins near the entrance for self-service.

3 Review the order of worship.
When seated, open the bulletin and find the order of the service, usually printed on the first or second page. Some churches print the entire service in the bulletin so worshipers don't have to switch back and forth between worship aids.

4 Determine if other worship resources are required.
The order of worship may specify additional hymnals, song sheets, candles, or other external supplies required during the service.

5 Fill out the attendance card.
A card may be located inside the bulletin or somewhere in your row. Fill it out completely. You may be asked to pass this card to an usher or to place it in the offering plate. Some congregations have attendance books for people to sign.

⑥ Reflect on bulletin artwork.
Covers often feature a drawing or design that corre-
sponds to the season of the church year or the day's
Bible verses. Examine the artwork and make a mental
note of its connection to the lessons or sermon.

⑦ Track your worship progress.
The bulletin will guide you through the liturgy, hymns,
and lessons as you worship and let you know where you
are at all times. If your ETA is twelve noon—as it is for
many congregations—the order of service can serve as an
informal clock. This is particularly important if the line
forms at your favorite restaurant at 12:10.

⑧ Watch for liturgical dialogues.
The bulletin may contain spoken parts of the liturgy
not found in the hymnal. The worship leader's parts
may be marked with a "P:" or "L:". The congregation's
responses may be marked with a "C:" and are often
printed in boldface type.

⑨ Identify the worship leaders and assistants.
The names of ushers, musicians, greeters, readers,
acolytes, and pastors usually can be found in the bulletin. Greet these people by name following the service.
Make good eye contact.

⑩ Review the printed announcements.
Community activities, calendars, and updates are
often listed in the back of the bulletin. Scan listings
during the spoken announcements or alas, when the
sermon is irretrievably boring.

⑪ Make good use of the bulletin after the service.
Some congregations re-use bulletins for later services.
Return the bulletin if possible. Recycling bins may also

If you choose not to save your worship bulletin, be sure to recycle it whenever possible.

be provided. If you wish, or unless otherwise instructed, you may take the bulletin home with you. It does not take long to gather an impressive collection of church bulletins. Even if you get to worship services only half the time, in a mere 50 years you can collect over twelve hundred bulletins. When you remodel, these can be used to paper the den.

Be Aware

• Bulletins often use letter or color codes to signify which hymnals should be used. Look for a key or legend that details this information. Commonly used hymnals in United Methodist congregations include *The United Methodist Hymnal, The Faith We Sing, The Cokesbury Hymnal*, and *Songs of Zion.* Some congregations now do not use hymnals, but project hymns (and other worship material) onto a screen.

- Many church secretaries and worship committees need help preparing the bulletin each week. You may want to volunteer to copy, fold, or assemble the bulletin for an upcoming service.

- Most congregations stand at certain times during worship, such as to honor Jesus' presence when the Gospel is read. Standing and sitting—even occasional kneeling—aren't for exercise. Rather, they're an important physical participation in worship that helps you focus on the meaning behind the action. If you are not sure about when to stand or sit, keep an eye on the folks in front of you. The invitation to sit, stand, or kneel is worded so persons who are not physically able to participate can still join in the spirit, if not the posture, of the moment.

HOW TO SING A HYMN

Hymn singing is a powerful United Methodist tradition. Part of the family has been known as "singing Methodists" and some have said United Methodists learn and express their theology most often by what they sing. One of the founders of the movement, Charles Wesley (1707–1788), wrote over 6,000 hymns. His brother John Wesley (1703–1791) gave directions for singing that still appear in *The United Methodist Hymnal*, including the advice "above all sing spiritually. Have an eye on God in every word you sing."

❶ Locate hymns in advance.

As you prepare for worship, consult the worship bulletin or the hymn board to find numbers for the day's hymns. Bookmark these pages in the hymnal using an offering envelope, attendance card, or the wrapper from a previously dispatched stick of chewing gum.

❷ Familiarize yourself with the hymns.

The hymnal often contains a ton of information about the hymn. Find the credits for author—words—and composer—music (usually at the bottom of the hymn). When was it written? The tune has a name of its own which is printed with the hymn. (Examples would be "Duke Street," "Finlandia," and "Wer Nur Den Lieden Gott." What clues do these names give you?) Many hymnals group hymns by category; the category might be theological or seasonal or topical. In some ways, the table of contents of *The United Methodist Hymnal* is an outline of United Methodist theology and practice.

❸ Figure out those mystery numbers.

Check to see if the hymnal has a series of small numbers at the bottom or top of the page. For example, you might see 11.11.11.5 or 87.98.87 or 77.77. Make some mental guesses as to what these numbers might be: shoe size of composer or score of the game when the hymn was written or mystical language from Revelation. In truth, these numbers count the meter, number of syllables, in each phrase of the hymn. (The hymnbook might even have a metrical index such as the one beginning on page 926 of *The United Methodist Hymnal*.) Armed with these data, a worship planner can move a hymn text from one tune to another with the same meter.

❹ Assist nearby visitors or children.
Using a hymnal can be confusing. If your neighbors seem disoriented, help them find the correct pages, or let them read from your book.

❺ Adopt a posture for best vocal performance.
Hold the hymnal away from your body at chest level. Place one hand under the spine of the binding, leaving the other hand free to turn the pages. Keep your chin up so your voice projects outward.

❻ Begin singing.
If the hymn is unfamiliar, sing the melody for the first verse. If you read music, explore the written harmony parts during the remaining verses. Loud-singing neighbors may or may not be in tune, so follow them with caution.

Support the hymnal's spine with one hand. Place the other on the open page.

7 Focus on the hymn's content.

Some of the lyrics may connect with a scripture reading of the day. Certain ones may be especially inspiring.

8 Avoid dreariness.

Hymns are sometimes sung in such a serious way that the congregation forgets to enjoy the music. Sing with energy and feeling.

Be Aware

- Hymnals are not just for use at church. Consider keeping a personal copy of your congregation's hymnal at home for further reference and study. Hymnals also make excellent baptism or confirmation gifts.

- Some hymns use words and phrases that are difficult to understand (such as, "Here I raise mine Ebenezer," from the hymn "Come, Thou Fount of Every Blessing"). Use a dictionary or a Bible with a concordance to clear up any uncertainty.

HOW TO SING A PRAISE SONG

Many United Methodist congregations have services in the style often called Praise & Worship (P&W), featuring guitars and drums. In these settings the words are typically displayed on large, multimedia projection screens.

❶ Follow the instructions of the song leader.
Someone in the praise band will invite the congregation to stand up, sit down, repeat certain sections, or divide into men's and women's vocal parts. Pay attention to this person to avoid getting off track.

❷ Learn the melody and song structure.
Pay special attention to the melody line sung by the band's lead vocalist. Praise & Worship songs can be tricky because they are rarely printed with notated sheet music and are sung differently from place to place.

❸ Sing along with gusto.
Once the melody has been introduced, join in the singing. When you're comfortable with the song, experiment with harmony parts.

❹ Avoid "zoning out."
Singing lyrics that are projected onto giant screens can result in a glazed-over facial expression. Avoid this by surveying the worship area, noticing paraments and liturgical symbols, and making eye contact with other people.

❺ Identify lyrical themes.
Determine if the song is being used as a confession, a prayer, a hymn of praise, or serves another purpose.

❻ Watch out for raised hands.
Some United Methodists emote while singing contempo-

rary Christian songs and may suddenly raise their hands in praise to God. Be sure to give these worshipers plenty of room to avoid losing your eyeglasses.

Be Aware

- United Methodist worship is highly participatory. The praise band is there to help you and the congregation to sing and participate in worship, not to perform a concert.
- There are no strict prohibitions in the United Methodist tradition against physical expression during worship.
- In fact, in the earliest days of the movement, outsiders thought the services a bit too exuberant and the acts of worship just a bit too lively.
- In some congregations, praise gestures will draw amused stares.

Beware of especially passionate worshipers who might raise their hands too quickly.

HOW TO LISTEN TO A SERMON

United Methodist believe God's Word comes to us through the sacraments and the preaching of Holy Scripture. Honoring God's Word, not to mention getting something out of church, includes diligent listening to the sermon and active mental participation.

❶ Review active listening skills.
While the listener in this case doesn't get to speak, the sermon is still a conversation. Make mental notes as you listen. Take notice of where and why you react and which emotions you experience.

❷ Take notes.
Note-taking promotes active listening and provides a good basis for later reflection. It also allows you to return to confusing or complicated parts at your own leisure. Some congregations provide space in the bulletin for notes. Jot down key words or interesting phrases. A sermon is more than just the presentation of information, so trying to follow in outline form will not always work.

Take notes to recall key images and get more out of the sermon.

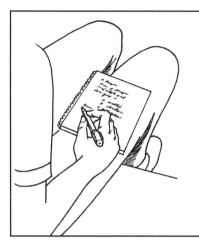

Alternative practices for listeners include: (a) making grocery lists, (b) sketching the person on the second row of the choir, (c) circling the "e's" in the bulletin, and (d) working through the alphabet, moving to the next letter each time the preacher uses a word beginning with a letter.

❸ Maintain good posture. Avoid slouching.

Sit upright with your feet planted firmly on the ground and your palms on your thighs, although it's a bit hard to do while taking notes. (See above.) Beware of the impulse to slouch, cross your arms, or lean against your neighbor, as these can encourage drowsiness.

❹ Listen for the hurting places.

You may feel an emotional pinch when the preacher names the sinner in you or the brokenness in our society. Pay attention to your reaction, and try to focus on waiting for the gospel rather than becoming defensive.

❺ Listen for the gospel.

This might well come in the form of a sentence starting with the name Jesus and ending with the words *for you*. Upon hearing the gospel, you may feel a physical lightness, as though you've set down a great burden. After all, it is called Good News! You may cry tears of joy. This is normal.

⑥ End by saying, "Amen."

Since preaching is mostly God's work, honor the Word by sealing the moment with this sacred word, which means, "It is most certainly true!"

⑦ Review and reflect.

If you've taken written notes, read through them later that day or the next day and consider corresponding with the preacher if you have questions or need clarification. If you've taken mental notes, review them in a quiet moment. Consider sharing this review time with others in your congregation or household on a weekly basis.

HOW TO RESPOND TO A DISRUPTION DURING WORSHIP

Disruptions during worship are inevitable. The goal is to soften their impact or perhaps to give meaning to their existence.

1 Simply ignore the offending event, if possible.
Many disruptions are brief and the persons involved act quickly to quiet them. Avoid embarrassing others; maintain your attention on the worship activity.

2 Some disruptions cannot be ignored and may threaten to continue indefinitely. The agony will go on unless you act. Consider the following types:

Active Children

- *Your Problem:* You are most familiar with your own family. If you sense an outburst will end quickly, simply allow it to pass. If not, escort the child to the lobby for a little quiet time, then return.

Try to ignore worship interruptions you think will end soon.

Note: Under all circumstances, children should be made to feel welcome in worship!

- *Someone Else's Problem:* Politely offer to help, perhaps by helping to occupy the child quietly or—with the parents' permission—by escorting the tot to the lobby, nursery, or cry room.

Personal Electronics

Turn off all personal electronic devices before worship.

- *Your Problem:* Turn off cell phones, pagers, and other electronic alarms immediately and discreetly. If contact is made and it is critical, remove yourself to the lobby and call back. Under no circumstances should you answer your phone during worship.

- *Someone Else's Problem:* Politely ask the person to respect worship by moving the conversation to the lobby. A friendly glare will probably do the trick. If someone seems greatly disturbed by a call received during the service, quietly ask "Can I help you?"

Chatty Neighbor

- *Your Problem:* Chatty persons should be alert to stares and grim looks from neighbors and be prepared to stop talking upon seeing them.

- *Someone Else's Problem:* Politely ask the talkers to wait until after worship to conclude the conversation. An alternative approach is to lean way over in the direction of the chatter as if you are eager to eavesdrop. If there is a coffee hour, be sure to approach the talkers with a cookie to mend any offense they may have felt.

Cameras

- *Your Problem:* Ask first if cameras are allowed. If so, unobtrusively and discreetly position yourself out of the line of sight of other worshipers. Be aware of the film's exposure number to avoid jarring auto-rewind noises. Flash cameras are *strictly* taboo.

- *Someone Else's Problem:* Politely offer to show the photographer where to stand to get the shot but without obstructing worship.

Sound System Feedback

- Pastors often make jokes to cover for feedback and keep the appropriate mood for worship. If this happens, consider making a donation earmarked for a "new sound system" in the plate.

Be Aware

- Some people may perceive tennis shoes with light-up soles on acolytes and other worship assistants to be disruptive. If possible, coordinate the color of the shoe lights with the season of the church year to avoid undue flak.

- Remember that crying babies are a sign of new life in the church. Keep in mind that those persons who talk during worship might be very lonely. Recognize that newcomers might not understand the culture of how your congregation worships. (Be grateful for new life, compassionate toward the lonely, and welcoming of the newcomer!)

THE ANATOMY OF A BAPTISM

United Methodists recognize three modes of baptism: sprinkling (water placed on the head of the person being baptized), pouring (water poured over the head), and immersion (going completely under water). The pastor will say, "*Name*, I baptize you in the name of the Father, and of the Son, and of the Holy Spirit."

God is the true actor in baptism, bringing everyone involved to the font and inspiring trust and faith.

Pastors preside at baptisms to ensure good order.

Sponsors (godparents) are sometimes on hand to support those being baptized and to make baptismal promises on behalf of children. The whole congregation joins in these promises and pledges its support also.

In some congregations, a baptismal candle is lit and presented to show that the newly baptized person has received the light of Christ.

Note: United Methodists baptize people of all ages—not just infants.

After the baptism with water, the pastor (and sometimes others) place hands on the forehead of the newly baptized and ask God's Holy Spirit to lead this person to be a faithful disciple of Jesus Christ. Baptism is initiation in the family of faith. It is a sign of God's grace claiming a life.

When children are baptized, their parents bring them to the font and make important promises to bring the child up in the Christian faith.

Water is the earthly element in baptism. God uses it to wash away sin and to drown the "old Adam" or "old Eve" in the baptized person. Water in itself can't do it— baptism is water connected to the power of God's word, and it is received by God's gift of faith.

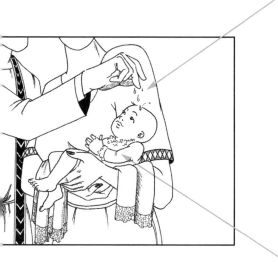

Baptism is received by a believing heart that trusts in God's word. In the case of infant baptism, the baptized person "borrows" one from his or her parents and congregation.

HOW TO RECEIVE COMMUNION

The Sacrament of Holy Communion (sometimes called the Lord's Supper, the Eucharist, or simply the Meal) is a central event in United Methodist worship. All five senses are engaged in Communion, and it is the most interactive part of the service. Local customs for receiving Communion can be confusing or complex, so it's wise to pay attention and prepare.

1 Determine which method of distribution is used.
Verbal directions or printed instructions will likely be given prior to the distribution. The three most common methods for Communion are *individual cups*, a *common cup*, or *intinction* (see pages 39–41).

Note: Some congregations commune in groups, usually kneeling at a prayer rail at the Table, and some practice "continuous Communion" with bread and cup stations, and some do both.

2 Look for guidance from the usher.
The usher will direct the people in each row or pew to stand and get in line. Many United Methodist congregations sing during the distribution of the elements.

3 Proceed to the Communion station.
Best practice is often simply to follow the person in front of you and do what they do. (If you happen to be following a child who is bouncing with excitement, you will want to choose your own degree of bouncing!)

4 Kneel, if appropriate.
Congregations that commune in groups or at "tables" often do so by instructing communicants to kneel at a

railing. When this happens, remember to stand slowly to avoid jostling your neighbor. Assist people who are elderly with prayer rail navigation when they need help.

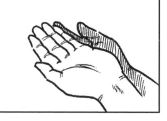

To receive the bread, make a "cross" or "cradle" with your hands, palms up.

Individual Cups

❶ Receive the bread.
When receiving the bread, place one upward palm on top of the other symbolically to make a "cross" or "cradle." After the server places the bread in your open hands, grasp the piece with the fingers of one hand. When the server says, "The body of Christ, given for you," eat the bread.

Note: Bread is commonly distributed in both baked or "loaf" form and in wafer form. Either is acceptable.

❷ Receive the cup.
Take a filled cup (or small glass) from the tray. When the server says, "The blood of Christ, given for you," drink from the cup.

❸ Return the empty cup.
A Communion assistant may follow the servers with a tray for the used cups. Deposit your empty cup. Many prayer rails have small round holes where the empty cup can be placed.

Common Cup

1 Receive the bread.
See previous page.

2 Receive the cup.
The grape juice will be
served in a large cup or
"chalice," as a sign of unity.
Assist the server by placing
one hand underneath the
cup and the other hand on
its side. Help the server
guide the cup to your lips.

3 Avoid leaving backwash.
Drink only one sip from the
common cup. Remove your
lips from the cup immedi-
ately after receiving the
juice.

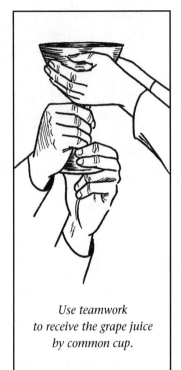

*Use teamwork
to receive the grape juice
by common cup.*

Intinction

Note: The word *intinction*
is from the Latin word *intingere*, which means "to dip."

1 Receive the bread.
Follow the same procedure as with individual cups and
common cup, but DO NOT EAT THE BREAD YET. If you
accidentally eat the bread prematurely, REMAIN CALM.
Simply ask for another piece.

❷ Receive the cup.

Position the bread you are holding over the cup. Grasp the bread tightly and dip just the edge of it into the juice. When the server says, "The blood of Christ given for you," eat the juice-soaked bread.

❸ Do not panic if you accidentally drop your bread into the cup.

Again, the server can provide you with more bread.

If the person distributing bread is too far away, the server may allow you to drink directly from the cup. Receiving only one element (bread *or* juice) traditionally counts as full participation in Communion.

Gently dip the bread in the cup for Communion by intinction.

Once You Have Communed

- *Return to your seat.* If Communion is distributed in one continuous line, you may immediately return to your pew.

  OR

- *Wait for the completion of the distribution.* If you're being served as a group at the prayer rail, you may need to wait until all other worshipers are served before returning to your seat. This is an appropriate time to close your eyes, pray, or listen to the Communion music.

- *Receive the post-Communion blessing.* When everyone has been served, the presiding minister may bless the group.

- *Continue to participate when seated.* After returning to your place, you may join the congregation in singing the remaining Communion hymns or pray in silence.

Be Aware

- United Methodist practice is to use the unfermented juice of the grape for Communion. Even though the liturgy or music may refer to wine, the expected element is grape juice. A few congregations, particularly in ecumenical settings, have chosen to use wine.

- Out of concern for persons with wheat-intolerance, some congregations offer gluten-free bread.

- After receiving the bread and cup, avoid saying, "Thank you" to the server. The body and blood are gifts from God. If you wish, a gentle "Amen" or "Thanks be to God" is appropriate.

- Although it is common that only baptized persons receive Communion, it is typical in United Methodist practice not to turn away anyone who responds to the invitation. Persons who are not communing may choose to come forward for a pastoral blessing.

HOW TO PASS THE PLATE

Passing the offering plate requires physical flexibility and an ability to adapt to differing practices. The offering is a practice that dates back to Old Testament times, linking money and personal finance directly to one's identity as a child of God. Giving of one's financial resources is an integral part of a healthy faith life.

❶ Pay close attention to instructions, if any.
The presiding minister may announce the method of offering, or instructions may be printed in the worship bulletin or projected on an overhead screen.

❷ Be alert for the plate's arrival at your row or pew.
Keep an eye on the ushers, if there are any. In most congregations, guiding and safeguarding the offering plate is their job, so wherever they are, so is the plate. As the plate approaches you, set aside other activity and prepare for passing.

❸ Avoid watching your neighbor or making judgments about their offering.
Many people contribute once a month by mail and some by automatic withdrawal from a bank account. If your neighbors pass the plate to you without placing an envelope, check, or cash in it, do not assume that they didn't contribute.

❹ Place your offering in the plate as you pass it politely to the next person.
Do not attempt to make change from the plate if your offering is in cash. If you are using an offering envelope (often found in a rack on the back of the pew in front of you) or giving a check, turn the envelope or check face down when you place it into the plate. Avoid letting the

plate rest in your lap as you finish writing a check. Simply pass it on and hand your check to an usher as you leave at the end of worship.

⑤ Be sensitive to idiosyncrasies in plate types.
Some congregations use traditional, wide-rimmed, felt-lined, brass-plated offering plates. Some use baskets of varying types. Some use cloth bags hung at the ends of long wooden poles that the ushers extend inward from the ends of the pews. (You will probably want to be a wee bit

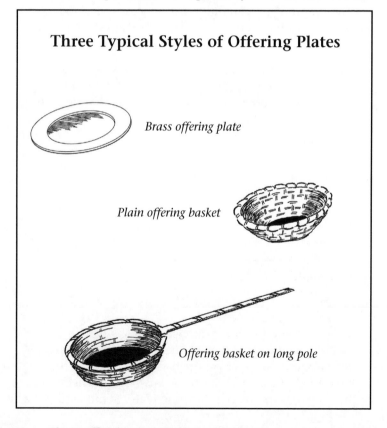

Three Typical Styles of Offering Plates

Brass offering plate

Plain offering basket

Offering basket on long pole

cautious if someone walks up the aisle taking money into hand and stuffing it directly into pocket.)

Be Aware

- Some congregations place the offering plate or basket at the rear of the worship space.

- Your church offering may be tax deductible, as provided by law. Consider making your offering by check or automatic withdrawal; most churches will send you a financial statement to be used (a) for tax purposes and (b) to help you evaluate your giving patterns.

- For financial resources, churches often depend entirely upon the money that comes in through congregational offerings. If you are a member, resolve to work yourself toward tithing as a putting-your-money-where-your-mouth-is expression of faith. (The term *tithing* means "one-tenth" and refers to the practice of giving 10 percent of one's gross income to support the church's work.)

- Everyone, regardless of their age, has something to offer.

- Offerings are not fees or dues given out of obligation. They are gifts of thanksgiving returned to God from the heart.

- After the offering is collected, most congregations join in an act of presentation, by standing to sing the Doxology and offering a prayer of dedication. If the Lord's Supper is to be celebrated, the Communion elements may be presented at this time.

- Sometimes, the offering plate is used to collect prayer requests, visitor cards, church meal reservations, and, in the case of frenetic children, used chewing gum wrappers and, in the case of frenetic adults, IOUs.

HOW TO SHARE THE PEACE IN CHURCH

In Romans 16:16, Paul tells members of the congregation to "greet one another with a holy kiss." The First Letter of Peter ends, "Greet one another with a kiss of love. Peace to all of you who are in Christ" (1 Peter 5:14).

Some United Methodists worry about this part of the worship service because of its free-for-all nature. (You may worship in some congregations who omit this "passing of the peace" entirely.) Some also feel uncomfortable because of their fear of being hugged. You can survive the peace, however, with these steps.

1 Adopt a peaceful frame of mind.
Clear your mind of distracting and disrupting thoughts so you can participate joyfully and reverently. The invitation is usually a call to offer one another signs of reconciliation and love.

2 Determine the appropriate form of safe touch.
Handshaking is most common. Be prepared, however, for hugs, half-hugs, one-armed hugs, pats, and other forms of physical contact. Nods are appropriate for distances greater than two pews or rows. In some settings, the congregation will scatter over the entire room to expand the greeting of peace.

3 Refrain from extraneous chitchat.
The sharing of the peace is not the time for lengthy introductions to new people, comments about the weather, or observations about yesterday's game. A brief encounter is appropriate, but save conversations for after this service.

Make good eye contact as you share God's peace with others.

④ Make appropriate eye contact.
Look the other person in the eye but do not stare.
The action of looking the person in the eye highlights
the relationship brothers and sisters in Christ have
with one another.

⑤ Declare the peace of God.
What should you say? "The peace of the Lord be with
you," "Peace be with you," "The peace of God," "God's
peace," and "The peace of Christ," are ways of speaking
the peace. Add the person's name, if you can. (Phrases
such as "you incompetent blockhead" and "you are theologically bankrupt" and "that dress makes you look fat"
are bad form.) Once spoken, the peace is there. Move on
to the next person.

Be Aware

• Safe touch involves contact that occurs within your
personal space but does not cause discomfort or unease.
Be sensitive to the fact that what is comfortable personal
space varies from person to person.

HOW TO STAY ALERT IN CHURCH

1 Get adequate sleep.
Late Saturday nights are Sunday morning's worst enemy. Resolve to turn in earlier.

2 Drink plenty of water, though not too much.
It is easier to remain alert when you are well hydrated.

3 Eat a high-protein breakfast.
Foods high in carbohydrates force your body to metabolize them into sugars, which can make you drowsy.

4 Arrive early and find the coffee pot.
If you don't drink coffee, consider a caffeinated soda.

5 Focus on your posture.
Sit up straight with your feet planted firmly on the floor. Avoid slouching, as this encourages sleepiness. Good posture will promote an alert bearing and assist in paying attention, so you'll get more out of worship and can give more to the worship of God.

6 If you have difficulty focusing on the service, divert your attention. Occupy your mind, not your hands.
Look around the worship space for visual stimuli. Keep your mind active in this way while continuing to listen.

7 Stay alert by flexing muscle groups in a pattern.
Clench toes and feet; flex calf muscles, thighs, glutei, abdomen, hands, arms, chest, and shoulders. Repeat. Avoid shaking, rocking, or other movements that attract undue attention.

⑧ If all else fails, consider pinching yourself.
Dig your nails into the fleshy part of your arm or leg, pinch yourself, bite down on your tongue with moderate pressure. Try not to cry out.

⑨ If perchance your head drops suddenly, try this.
Quickly reach for a pencil and make notes (about anything) so as to give inkling that you lowered your head only to write down some important point.

⑩ If, alas, you do doze off, be sure to look heavenward.
Whisper "Amen" when your eyes finally open. Neighbors might even be impressed with your public piety.

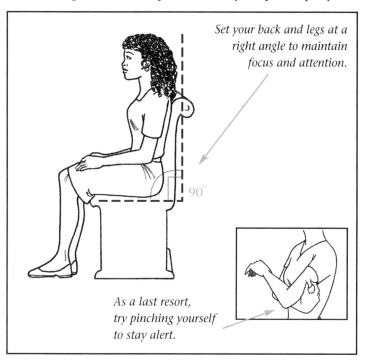

Set your back and legs at a right angle to maintain focus and attention.

90°

As a last resort, try pinching yourself to stay alert.

WHAT TO BRING TO A CHURCH POTLUCK (BY REGION)

It is a generally followed practice in North American churches to enjoy three courses at potlucks (commonly referred to as "dishes"). Many of these dishes take on the flavor of the regions or cultures they represent. For best results, the preparer should understand the context in which the "dish" is presented.

The term "potluck" is used here as a generic expression for what some folks call a covered dish meal, group picnic, surprise supper, stone soup, smorgasbord, bring-a-plate, Jacob's join, join-in meal, or who-brought-that supper.

The Salad

Potluck salads are quite different from actual salads. In preparation for making a potluck salad, ask yourself three questions:

- Is this dish mostly meat-free?
- Can this dish be served with a spoon or salad tongs?
- Can it be served chilled?

If the answer is "yes" to any of these questions, consider the dish a potluck-eligible salad.

The Mixture

This is the foundation of any potluck salad. It gives the salad a sense of direction. If at all possible, use ingredients that are indigenous to your area. For example, broccoli, lettuce, apples, macaroni, and candy bars are common in more temperate climates.

The Crunchy Stuff

This component gives life and pizzazz to an otherwise bland salad. Examples: tortilla chips, shoestring potato crisps, onion crisps, and fried pigskins. To be frowned upon are the use of actual shoestrings or the substitution of footballs for pigskins.

The Glue

The glue holds the salad together. The variety of available types is stunning, ranging from a traditional oil-based salad dressing to mayonnaise and non-dairy whipped topping. Use your imagination. Consult regional recipes for exact ingredients.

Note: Some salads are best when made well in advance and allowed to sit overnight. This is called *marinating*, or "controlled decomposition." Do not use actual glue adhesive. Other salads are best prepared immediately before serving.

The Casserole

A three-layered dish, typically. In order to make each casserole as culturally relevant as possible, use the following guidelines. Consult local restaurants for ideas, when in doubt. If you are not regionally offended when reading these stereotypes, you are probably not reading closely enough.

Starch

East Coast: pasta or rice pilaf

Midwest: rice, potatoes, noodles, or more rice

South: grits

Southwest: black, red, or pinto beans

West Coast: tofu

Meat

East Coast: sausage or pheasant

Midwest: ground beef—in a pinch, SPAM® luncheon meat

South: crawdad or marlin

Southwest: pulled pork

West Coast: tofu

Cereal

East Coast: corn flakes

Midwest: corn flakes

South: corn flakes

Southwest: corn flakes

West Coast: tofu flakes

Note: The starch and meat may be mixed with a cream-based soup. The cereal must always be placed on the top of the casserole.

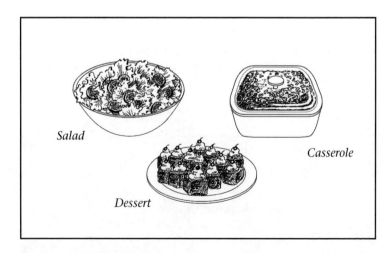

Salad

Casserole

Dessert

The Dessert

The most highly valued dish at a potluck, this can be the simplest and most fun to make. There are two key ingredients:

1. flour
2. fudge

Regional influences can be quite profound. The following are examples of typical desserts around the country. Consult your church's seniors for the nuances of your region.

Cleveland: fudge brownies with fudge frosting

Kansas City: triple-fudge fudge with fudge sauce and a side of fudge

Los Angeles: tofu fudge

Miami: fudge

New York City: cheesecake with fudge drizzle

Be Aware

*   Use caution when preparing a dish. Adding local ingredients to any meat, salad, or dessert can increase the fellowship factor of your potluck exponentially. It also raises the risk of a "flop."

*   Always follow safe food-handling guidelines.

*   Any combination of flavored gelatin, shredded carrots, mini-marshmallows, and canned pears is an acceptable "utility" dish, should you be unable to prepare one from the above categories.

*   To compliment a dish (or to solve the mystery of what you just ate), simply say, "Oh, could I have the recipe?" If you are not sure yourself as to what you threw into the dish, reply, "Thanks, but it's a family secret."

HOW TO LEARN AND GROW

United Methodists have numerous settings designed to help persons grow in God's grace, settings for learning and spiritual enrichment.

One of the very first Sunday Schools was started by a Methodist in England. Local churches still offer study groups of all shapes and sizes. Small groups develop to support members. (For example, Disciple Bible study, Companions in Christ, and Sisters are ministries created by The United Methodist Church for in-depth Bible study, spiritual accountability, and mutual caring.)

United Methodist congregations often have gender-specific and age-specific groups (United Methodist Women, United Methodist Men, United Methodist Youth, for example). Program activities extend from everything from softball to movies to exercise to prayer to healing to fund-raisers to visitation to retreats to 12-step groups to . . . you name it.

In a typical United Methodist congregation (Is there such a thing!), almost half of the members participate in some level of church school.

Do not be surprised to learn:

- The Fellowship Class probably split off from the Friendship Class because the members did not like each other.
- It's hard to find a teacher for the eighth-grade boys.
- The average age in the Young Men's Bible Class is approximately 80.
- The Susie B. Von Snook Class has met in the same room for 46 years and still does not allow the youth to eat potato chips there.

- The pictures in the kindergarten classroom are hung at a height of six feet, while most of the class members are about three feet high.

  But then, also don't be surprised to learn:

- Members really care for one another and are concerned when someone is home sick.

- Members want to relate the Bible to the world in which they live (and relate the world in which they live to the Bible).

- Members welcome newcomers.

- Members remember favorite teachers from years ago.

- Members trust each other enough to disagree with one another.

- Members enjoy the presence of the Holy Spirit making Jesus present as the Teacher and Savior.

  What happens in an adult Sunday School class?

- The class often has an informal gathering time to catch up with one another and perhaps to enjoy a cup of coffee. Study time might be 10 or 15 minutes later than starting time!

- In formal or informal ways, class members get the names of those who are sick or out of town or who have new grandchildren or who have just moved into the community or who are needed for the upcoming church fund-raising stew.

- Some classes take up a class offering for class projects, study materials, general Sunday School expenses, cards for the ill, or simply because they have always taken up an offering. This offering is not to be confused with the offering gathered at the worship service.

- Some classes have a teacher who leads each week. Other classes have a rotation of teachers. Some classes lead themselves in a discussion format. The choices of study resources vary, although many United Methodist groups get their materials from Cokesbury/Abingdon Press, the denominational publisher.

- Classes often have a traditional opening prayer or Scripture verse and frequently close with an established class benediction. Because these are usually spoken while eyes are closed, the stranger need not fear others will notice that he or she is really mumbling a word or two behind the pace of the others.

- Church school groups (children, youth, and adult) may meet outside the regularly scheduled meeting. Work projects, class parties, service activities, and meals together provide an extension of class fellowship.

- If you do not find a church school group that scratches your itch (or blows your horn or warms your goose bumps), start one yourself. To do so is not just about making sure things fit your particular need (that could tend toward selfishness); it is also about expanding the ministry of the church to others (that could tend toward service).

FIVE FAMOUS FOLKS OF FAITH FREQUENTLY FOUND FRIENDLY

The United Methodist Church around the world has around 10,000,000 members (about 8,000,000 of them in the United States). Before the present crop of United Methodists, there have been millions and millions more. Here are five of those multimillions who are often named as the founders of this family of faith. And usually found friendly.

To deflect family feuds, these are listed by last name in alphabetical order.

❶ Jacob Albright (1759–1808)

Working in Pennsylvania as a farmer and a tile maker (known for his honesty and integrity), Albright grew in his religious conviction that faith was more than correct form. True faith changed the way one lived. Although he cooperated with English-speaking Methodist preachers, his ministry emerged chiefly among German-speaking people. Eventually, the religious societies which formed from his work emerged as the Evangelical Church.

❷ Martin Boehm (1725–1812)

Boehm was a farmer who practiced the Mennonite faith. One of the observances of that tradition was to choose pastors by lot (perhaps by drawing straws, the one with the longest straw being named pastor). The community felt this custom allowed God to choose whom God would have as pastor. Boehm, although untrained, was thus picked as pastor. As he grew into that role, his religious passion increased. He preached in Pennsylvania and his evangelistic mission led to the founding of the Church of the United Brethren in Christ.

❸ Philip William Otterbein (1726–1813)

At the age of 26, Otterbein responded to a call to leave Germany to minister to German-speaking persons in America. Highly educated in the Reformed tradition, Otterbein was close to the patterns and teachings of early Methodism in this country. He helped spark a revival movement, insisted on the highest moral standards of conduct, and organized groups for growth and accountability. Otterbein (along with Boehm) was instrumental in the establishment of the Church of the United Brethren in Christ.

❹ Charles Wesley (1707–1788)

During his university days at Oxford, he was central in the founding of a group (now called "the Holy Club") that emphasized Bible study, service, devout living, disciplined accountability, and regular participation in the Lord's Supper. He became a priest in the Church of England. With his brother John, he was a key part of the Methodist reform movement in England. His gifts as a poet and musician were expressed in over 6,000 hymns. Those hymns provide an accessible form of theology and doctrine.

❺ John Wesley (1703–1791)

John Wesley's effort to bring an evangelistic and sacramental revival to the Church of England (he was a priest in that church) led to a Methodist movement within the Anglican church. At the time of the American Revolution, John Wesley saw the need for an American Methodist church independent of the English parent. He supported and helped to shape the organization in 1784 of The Methodist Episcopal Church in America.

TANTALIZING TRUE TRIVIA TELLING TONS ABOUT THESE FOUNDERS OF MOVEMENTS

The knowledge of the following will enable you to amuse and amaze your friends—if you have any after you tell them all these tantalizing true trivia.

- John Wesley opposed the independence of the American colonies.
- John and Charles Wesley had 17 brothers and sisters.
- Philip William Otterbein had a twin who died a few weeks after birth.
- Jacob Albright had several of his children to die in one year because of dysentery (diarrhea).
- John Wesley was most unhappy in his marriage.
- Philip William Otterbein loved to grow flowers.
- Martin Boehm's son was a leader in the Methodist movement.
- Martin Boehm as a farmer owned over 400 acres of productive crop land.
- Charles Wesley dearly loved the family's pet cat.
- Jacob Albright almost died from illnesses on numerous occasions.
- Philip William Otterbein served a church in Baltimore that is now immediately adjacent to Camden Yards where the Baltimore Orioles play baseball.
- John Wesley averaged taking Communion four times a week.

- Jacob Albright would pray at least an hour before he preached.

- Martin Boehm was said to be short and stout.

- John Wesley was five feet, three inches, and weighed 126 pounds.

- Philip William Otterbein asked that his sermons be destroyed upon his death.

- Jacob Albright often hummed or sang hymns as he walked.

- Martin Boehm's father came to America to escape religious persecution in Europe.

- Charles Wesley left home when eight years old in order to attend boarding school.

John Wesley

A FEW IMPORTANT THINGS SAID BY A FEW IMPORTANT PEOPLE IN A FEW IMPORTANT SITUATIONS (INCLUDING A CURE FOR BALDNESS)

John Wesley came close to having no unpublished thoughts. What he thought, he wrote. What he wrote, he published. Charles Wesley, John's brother, wrote over 6,000 hymns. Some of them seem pretty bad ("Ah! The Lovely Appearance of Death!"). Most of them are quite good ("O for a Thousand Tongues to Sing!"). What he thought, he wrote. What he wrote, he sang.

Because the Wesley brothers were so prolific, United Methodists sometimes are tempted to turn only to them for the early written insights of United Methodism. Philip William Otterbein and Martin Boehm and Jacob Albright preached and taught widely, but they did not put much into publication. If these quotations tend to draw chiefly from the Wesleys, it is because so much of their writing is still in print.

❶ "Our main doctrines, which include all the rest, are three, that of repentance, of faith, and of holiness. The first of these we account, as it were, the porch of religion; the next, the door; the third, religion, itself."

—John Wesley, "*The Principles of a Methodist Farther Explained*" (1746)

Here John Wesley (in an ongoing written debate with a Mr. Church, a vicar in the Church of England) is teaching that the principal fruit of faith is holy living (sanctification). The evidence of authentic faith is a life lived with love of God and love of neighbor. "Getting saved" does not end at the prayer rail. Salvation's journey goes right into the middle of daily living.

❷ "The gospel demands, but it also gives what it demands."

> —Philip William Otterbein, *"The Salvation Bringing and Glorious Incarnation . . . "* (1760)

Otterbein, in one of the few of his sermons still available, has stated the great theme of United Methodism—grace, God's freely given, undeserved rescue of those who accept God's offer of love.

I felt my heart strangely warmed

John Wesley, Aldersgate Street meeting.

❸ "I felt my heart strangely warmed. I felt I did trust in Christ, Christ alone for salvation, and an assurance was given me that he had taken away my sins, even mine, and saved me from the law of sin and death."

> —John Wesley, *Journal* (1738)

One distinctive emphasis in Wesleyan theology is the doctrine of assurance. In this beloved quotation, John

Wesley describes what happened at a meeting he attended on Aldersgate Street in London, May 24, 1738. Although Wesley's opinion changed from time to time, he remained clear that ordinarily God gives the gift of assurance to those who are saved from sin.

❹ "After I had experienced the grace of regeneration, I soon recognized the fact that the surest and best way to work out my soul's salvation, and to be ready at all times to fight the good fight of faith was, to be in fellowship with devout Christians, and to take part in bearing the cross, to pray for and with one another, to be vigilant and edify each other by means of an exemplary life in service of God."

—Jacob Albright, quoted in *Leben Erfahrung und Amtsführung Zweyer Evangelischer Prediger Jakob Albrecht und Georg Miller* (1834)

Albright expressed a core principle of United Methodism: the life of faith is lived in community. (John Wesley once said in effect "Solitary Christian is a contradiction in terms.") The earliest group organized by Albright was called a Connection. United Methodism still sees itself as a connectional movement of interactive relationships. No individual and no congregation stands alone. We are in this together.

❺ "But even though (the early church) did celebrate the Eucharist every day, yet they looked upon the Lord's Day as a time when they were more particularly obliged to administer it . . . Indeed, if we consider the name of the Lord's Day we shall scarcely be able to assign a better reason for its being called so, than because it was constantly celebrated with the Lord's Supper which was in those early days of Christianity looked upon as the necessary distinguishing service . . . the omission of which was accounted the greatest profanation of the holy festival that could be imagined or supposed."

—Charles Wesley, *Sermons* (1748)

In this sermon, Charles Wesley is arguing for the early Methodist practice of constant Communion. (The 2004 General Conference of The United Methodist Church asked local churches to consider having Communion at the main service of worship each week.) At the time of the Methodist evangelistic revival in England, the Church of England had lost its fervor for Holy Communion and part of the energy of the Wesleys was to restore that sacrament to a central place in the community of faith.

❻ "(I) pray for grace to teach others the way to salvation, and (I) have not prayed for (my) own salvation. Lost! Lost! Lord, save, I am lost! (I heard the words of Jesus): 'I am come to seek and save that which is lost.' In a moment, a stream of joy poured over me."

—Martin Boehm (1758)

In Martin Boehm's account of his life changing experience, there are several matters of United Methodist teaching: (a) Jesus seeks out the lost (called "prevenient grace," a grace which is working in us before we know it); (b) each person must admit his or her need for a Savior; (c) a personal encounter with Jesus changes one's life; (d) often, God also gives the joy of the assurance of salvation. For some persons, this gift of new birth occurs in an instant (as it did for Martin Boehm). For other persons, the "pregnancy" for the new birth is more gradual.

❼ "(Cure for) Raging Madness: Apply to the head, cloths dipped in cold water. Or, set the patient with his head under a great water fall, as long as his strength will bear, or pour water on his head out of a tea kettle. Or, let him eat nothing but apples for a month. Or, nothing but bread and milk . . . Keep the head close shaved, and frequently wash it with vinegar."

—John Wesley, *Primitive Physic or An Easy and Natural Method of Curing Most Diseases* (1780)

Although these helps for mental illness seem strange to twenty-first century readers, they represent John Wesley's conviction that God is concerned about all of life, body as well as soul. John Wesley also had a special concern that the poor did not have the same access to physicians as did the wealthy, so he produced several editions of *Primitive Physic* in an effort to assure poor people some quality of medical attention. His hints cover topics ranging from toothache to cancer to obesity (a diet of turnips or carrots) to dog bites to a cure for baldness (applying rosemary to the scalp) to gout. These practices planted the seeds of United Methodist social ministries.

❽ "I look upon all the world as my parish; thus far, I mean in whatever part of it I am, I judge it meet, right, and my bounden duty to declare unto all that are willing to hear the glad tiding of salvation. This is the work which I know God has called me to. And sure I am that his blessing attends it."

—John Wesley, *Letters* (1739)

Some of John Wesley's contemporaries thought he violated church decorum, if indeed not ecclesiastical law, by preaching in parishes assigned to other priests. In this letter, Mr. Wesley spells out his broader view of the evangelistic task, a work that has no boundary of region or nation or race. United Methodism in the twenty-first century continues to think of the gospel as a universal gospel.

SOME THINGS IT WON'T HURT YOU TO KNOW ABOUT HOW UNITED METHODISM CAME INTO BEING*

If history is not "your thing," at least skim the topics here and pause where something grabs your interest.

❶ Adam and Eve

However humanity came into being, United Methodists fall into the general category of human beings, so our history begins with creation. Today, most United Methodists are still human beings (which means that there is enough sin to go around).

❷ Abraham, Sarah, Moses, Miriam

United Methodists trace their faith roots through the heroes and heroines (and lesser lights) of the Old Testament. The faith family tree has decidedly Jewish roots.

❸ Jesus Christ

The United Methodist story goes through (and is transformed by) the life, death, resurrection, ascension, and promised final reign of Jesus Christ. Faithfulness to that relationship is the standard for testing United Methodist history.

❹ Paul, Deborah, Timothy, Tychicus, Aristarchus

United Methodism, when at its best, shapes life in keeping with the commitments and values of the New

---

* Including a few things that will help you sleep better at night, create for you a massive personal fortune, and teach you a foreign language in ten easy lessons. Of course, this is not a legal promise.

Testament church. Most United Methodists do not speak Greek, wear sandals, or know who Aristarchus was, but seek, in other ways, to be a New Testament church.

⑤ St. Ignatius, St. Polycarp, Justin Martyr, Tertullian, Origen, Hippolytus
Some United Methodists do not remember to claim these second- and third-century teachers and leaders as part of the United Methodist chronicle. "Aren't they Roman Catholic?" Yes, but our narrative has more years as Roman Catholic than as Protestant!

⑥ Constantine (fourth century)
In 312, Emperor Constantine won a great military battle following a dream that told him to fight under the sign of the cross. He stopped persecution of Christians and, near his death, was himself baptized. Later, at the end of the fourth century, Christianity became the official state religion of the Roman Empire.

⑦ Middle Ages, Orthodox Church, Crusades (391–1517)
Ecumenical church councils began to agree on basic Christian doctrine (the Trinity, for example). St. Augustine and St. Patrick were active. The Orthodox Church split from the Roman Catholic Church. The horrors of the Crusades were done in the name of the church. (For better and for worse, these are ancestral cousins of United Methodists.)

In the midst of this exciting story, we take a brief commercial break to consider five facts about life in medieval times.

Five Facts about Life in Medieval Times.

• It lasted more than 1,000 years. By some counts, the medieval period (or Middle Ages) covered an era that began around the year 391 (when Christianity became the Roman Empire's only legal religion) and ended around 1517 (the year Martin Luther wrote the Ninety-five Theses).

- Life was nasty, brutish, and short. People who survived childhood usually did not live long past age 40. If disease or starvation didn't get you, violence and warfare did. It's been estimated that during the 1400s about one-third of Europe's population died of bubonic plague. Sanitation was practically non-existent.

- The Christian church grew larger, more influential, and more dominant. Headquartered in Rome, the Western church became a superpower. Church and state became inseparable. At its height (ca. 1000–1300), "Christian Crusaders" battled with Muslims and others for control

Road travel was harsh and sanitation was minimal during the Middle Ages.

of the "Holy Land," Thomas Aquinas wrote his *Summa Theologica*, and hundreds of "heretics" were burned to death.

- The "Cult of the Saints" developed. Over the centuries, a system grew in which the leftover good works (merits) of the saints could be distributed to others, with the pope in charge of this store (treasury) of good works. With his Ninety-five Theses, Luther challenged this system.

- Humanist and Renaissance-age thinkers also worked for reform. At the end of the Middle Ages, early reformers such as Jan Hus and Girolamo Savonarola confronted the church corruptions they saw. Hus was burned, and Savonarola was hanged. For other examples, see "History's Six Most Notorious Heretics" a few pages over. All right! If you cannot wait, go ahead and read about heretics now, but let's agree to meet back here in, say, ten minutes.

Now, continuing on after our brief interlude.

❽ Martin Luther, 1517

A German Roman Catholic monk, Martin Luther challenged abuses within the church. Those who followed him were called "Protestants," both in the sense of protesting wrongs and in the sense of proclaiming a gospel centered on faith (as opposed to good works). With the emergence of the Lutheran Reformation, United Methodism's thread began to move primarily in the Protestant tradition. Want to know more? Read on.

Five Things to Know about the Reformation.

- Most people in medieval times had low expectations. They didn't know anything about advanced medicine, modern psychology, or what it was like to live in a democracy. They didn't expect to live very long. They didn't think they had much power over their lives. And they didn't think being an "individual" was very important.

- The reformers were Roman Catholic. The reformers wanted to make changes within the one Christian church in Europe, but they wanted to stay Catholic. None of them ever expected that their actions would lead to the dozens of Christian denominations around today.

Lutherans, United Methodists, and other non-Lutherans credit Martin Luther (1483–1546) for spearheading the Reformation.

- People in medieval times weren't allowed to choose their own religion. You could believe whatever you wanted, but you could only practice the faith your prince or king chose. After the Reformation, only the regions whose princes had signed the Augsburg Confession could practice any faith other than Catholicism.

- Martin Luther wasn't the only reformer. Luther wanted the church to rediscover the good news of Jesus that creates and restores faith. Other reformers fought for these changes: separation of church and state, a personal relationship with God, better-educated priests, and more moral leaders in the church.

- Luther wrote down 95 theses he wanted to debate. In 1517, in keeping with the custom of the day, Luther nailed his debating points to the church door in Wittenberg, Germany. The feathers began to fly. Church and political leaders attacked him. He refused to recant. ("Here I stand. I can do no other.") Other reformers joined Luther and the Protestant Reformation took a life of its own. The German roots of United Methodism (remember Otterbein, Boehm, Albright?) were being fed.

Continuing again with the story of how United Methodism came into being:

⑨ Church of England, 1534

King Henry VIII, unable to get the Pope to dissolve Henry's marriage, had himself declared head of a national church in England. The Church of England (Anglican Church) took its theology chiefly from the Protestant strain of the church, but retained much of the liturgical language and practice of the Roman Catholic Church. In 1549, the Church of England released *The Book of Common Prayer*, its official service book. John and Charles Wesley were priests in the Church of England and within that tradition unfolded the Methodist revival movement, seeking to recover a sacramental life and an evangelistic life for the church.

⑩ Aldersgate Street, 1738

May 24, 1738 is a date still remembered in United Methodism (Aldersgate Sunday is the Sunday nearest the 24th). On that date, John Wesley attended a prayer meeting-Bible Study, probably sponsored by Moravians. As someone was reading what Martin Luther had written about the book of Romans, Wesley felt a fresh and powerful assurance that God's gift of salvation was for him.

⑪ Otterbein and Boehm, 1767

The erudite Otterbein and the plain Boehm both ministered among German-speaking people. When Otterbein heard Boehm preach (at Isaac Long's barn near Lancaster, Pennsylvania), he embraced him and exclaimed, "Wir sind Brüder!" (We are brethren!) Their relationship later gave vigor to the emergence of the United Brethren in Christ.

⑫ American Methodism, 1784

As immigrants came to the American colonies, some of them brought with them their Methodist convictions. Although Methodism in America was a lay movement (Francis Asbury, Robert Strawbridge, Barbara Heck, Harry Hosier, Thomas Webb, Philip Embury), its leaders recognized the need for clergy, to bring order and to offer the sacraments. At a Christmas conference in 1784, in Baltimore, The Methodist Episcopal Church in America was organized. (Philip William Otterbein was there to help set apart Francis Asbury as a bishop.)

⑬ United Brethren in Christ Church, 1800

German-speaking preachers such as George Adam Geeting, John Neidig, John George Pfrimmer, and Christian Newcomer joined with their leaders, Philip William Otterbein and Martin Boehm, to form the United Brethren in Christ Church. In establishing their own *Book of Discipline*, they found much upon which to draw in the Methodist edition.

⑭ The Evangelical Association, 1803

As the classes and societies formed by Jacob Albright began to grow, Albright recognized the need to bring order to the ministry and to conserve the spiritual gains of the work. Other leaders include John Walter, Peter Walter, George Miller, and Samuel Liesser. They made formal organization in 1803 and committed themselves to follow the Scriptures as the guide and rule of faith. Albright had been influenced by a lay Methodist preacher, so it is not surprising that the early *Book of Discipline* was patterned after the Methodist volume.

⑮ Division in the Family, 1830, 1845, 1889, 1894

From time to time, separations came in the Methodist, United Brethren, and Evangelical households. Among these parting of the ways was the organization of the Methodist Protestant Church in 1830 (issues including role of laity and bishops); the establishment of the Methodist Episcopal Church, South, in 1845 (issues including church polity and slavery); the United Brethren in Christ—Old Constitution became separate in 1889 (issues chiefly around a revised Constitution; of interest is that one of the bishops who helped form UBC—Old Constitution was Milton Wright, father of Orville and Wilbur Wright, first to fly an airplane); in 1894, the United Evangelical Church emerged (issues included role of bishops, role of laity, and some personal rivalries). Remember, all this started a few pages back with Adam and Eve!

⑯ The Evangelical Church, 1922

The division between the Evangelical Association and the United Evangelical Church was healed, forming The Evangelical Church. It is significant that some of the leaders at the time of separation were principals in the reunion. One statement said, "Thus has been fulfilled a prophecy . . . This is also the consummation of a hope . . . the answer to prayer . . . the glorification of the Great Head of the Church."

⑰ The Methodist Church, 1939

The reunification of three branches of Methodism took place in 1939 when the Methodist Episcopal Church, the Methodist Episcopal Church, South, and the Methodist Protestant Church formed The Methodist Church. One price of the union was the establishment of a separate jurisdiction for Black members. Three major Black Methodist denominations had arisen from earlier racial divides: the African Methodist Episcopal Church (AME), the African Methodist Episcopal, Zion, Church (AMEZ), and the Christian Methodist Episcopal Church (CME).

⑱ The Evangelical United Brethren Church, 1946

The Evangelical Church and the United Brethren Church celebrated their common heritage among German-speaking people, recognized their similarities in theology, agreed on corresponding books of church life *(Book of Discipline)*, and in November 1946 merged into a new denomination, The Evangelical United Brethren Church.

⑲ The United Methodist Church, 1968

In May 1968 in Dallas, Texas, the Evangelical United Brethren and The Methodist Church came together to form The United Methodist Church. Thus was brought under one roof their German and English roots, their common missional foci, their commitments to evangelism, their almost parallel *Book of Discipline*, their mutual ecumenical interests, their theological and doctrinal emphases, and their sacramental lives. The separate Black jurisdiction of The Methodist Church was abolished and all members in both the Evangelical United Brethren (EUB) and the Methodist traditions shared in the gifts given to and given through this new household, The United Methodist Church.

Symbols and signs are ways of representing or marking a presence. Sometimes such insignia announce actual physical presence (golden arches do that) and sometimes such insignia tell of an abstract or institutional presence (the American flag does that). United Methodist colleges and universities, for example, are known by quite an array of athletic team symbols: Blue Devils (Duke), Orange (Syracuse), Mustangs (Southern Methodist), Panthers (Claflin), Lions (Albright), Terriers (Boston), Battling Bishops (Ohio Wesleyan), Cardinals (Otterbein), and Eagles (Emory). This is quite an assortment of zoo creatures, theological terrors, and color selection to be thrown at the opposition (and radically defended by the home base).

By what insignia has The United Methodist Church presented itself to the world? (Some folks might think that "devils" or "battling bishops" would be ideal representation of United Methodism, but that is only in lesser moments.)

The predecessor denominations (The Evangelical United Brethren Church and The Methodist Church) developed symbols, one official, one unofficial.

The Evangelical United Brethren symbol centered on a prominent cross, in front of which two hands clasp, bringing to mind the handshake of Bishop Clippinger and Bishop Stamm when the United Brethren and the Evangelical Church united in 1946.

The Methodist Church did not adopt an official logo but made wide use of what was called the "World Parish Cross," recalling John Wesley's statement that "The world is my parish."

Part of the Plan of Union for The United Methodist Church called for an official denominational symbol. The result was the familiar cross and flame.

- The design is now seen on church buildings, bulletins, tee shirts, coffee mugs, websites, calling cards, stationery, stained glass, tombstones, book covers, clergy stoles, directional signs, and, perhaps, on socks and lamp shades. Can you say "ubiquitous"? The cross and flame is a registered service mark and its use is limited to official United Methodist entities. (The General Council and Finance and Administration has to approve any commercial usage.)

- In this insigne, the cross of Christ is touched by the flame of the Holy Spirit. This design merges the core Christian understanding of the centrality of the death and resurrection of Jesus with the Wesleyan emphasis on the work of the Holy Spirit. Theologically, here is justification and sanctification. With the name of the denomination drawn into the symbol, the church is related to

God the Father through Jesus Christ and the Holy Spirit, a Trinitarian claim.

- The flames are reminders of Pentecost (Acts 2:3) and a call to renew the work of evangelism as the Spirit moves. The two tongues of fire blend to form one flame, offering the hope that the 1968 merger of The Methodist Church and The Evangelical United Brethren Church would blaze with the combined gifts of two traditions.

- Caution: Some very active and involved United Methodists, with a great love for the denomination, report rapid palpitations of the heart upon spotting the cross and flame mark. Some, as they travel around the country, have even programmed their GPS systems to locate the nearest cross and flame. Because the emblem is used worldwide by United Methodists, this caution should be packed with your passport.

HISTORY'S SIX MOST NOTORIOUS HERETICS

Though vilified by those who write history, heretics played a critical role in the church. They refined its message and forced the church to be honest with itself. But heretics usually paid the ultimate price, and often they were wrong. There is a space at the end of this section for you to enter an account of your favorite heretic. If you are your own favorite heretic, pay particular attention to the next section, "How to Avoid Getting Burned at the Stake."

❶ Hypatia of Alexandria (370–415)
Hypatia was an African philosopher, mathematician, physicist, astronomer, and director of Alexandria's Library, once the largest in the world. Bishop Cyril of Alexandria, out of jealousy, declared her a heretic and ordered her to be tortured and burned at the stake, together with her writings. Her mistakes were to prefer study to marriage, to know more than the bishop, and to be a female teacher of males.

❷ Pelagius (354–418)
Pelagius was a Celtic monk who believed in the goodness of human nature and the freedom of human will. These beliefs led him to denounce the doctrine of original sin—a core tenet of the church—and suggest that human beings were equal participants in their salvation with Jesus Christ. The *Pelagianism* movement, named after him, was a strict teaching of self-reliance. When Pelagius taught that one could achieve grace without the church, he was excommunicated.

❸ Joan of Arc (1412–1431)
Joan was a French peasant girl who was able to hear heavenly voices that urged her to liberate her nation from

the British occupation. She was 19 when sentenced as a heretic and burned at the stake. Joan's fault was to be a better army leader than men. She is now a national heroine.

④ Girolamo Savonarola (1452–1498)

His parents wanted him to be a physician, but this Italian youngster decided to be a Dominican monk and serve people who were poor. He preached against Pope Alexander VI and the powerful Medici family. Members of the wealthy church and society hanged and burned him, then threw his ashes into the Arno River to prevent him from having a restful place.

⑤ Martin Luther (1483–1546)

His father, a peasant and coal miner, wanted him to be a lawyer. Martin disappointed him and became an Augustinian monk. Because of Luther's challenge to some church practices, Emperor Charles V and Pope Leo X threw him out of the church and put a price on his head, but Luther continued serving the poor, preaching and living the Bible, and sharing hospitality at the family dinner table.

⑥ Hatuey (?–1511)

This Native American leader from the Guahaba region escaped from Haiti to Cuba. The brave Hatuey was captured and declared a heretic. A priest wanted to baptize him in order for the Indian to get to heaven after being burnt. The Taíno chief rejected the Christian rite when he heard that in heaven there would also be people from Spain.

⑦ Your favorite heretic:

_____

HOW TO AVOID GETTING BURNED AT THE STAKE

Burning at the stake has a centuries-long history as punishment for heretics. (A heretic is someone who challenges established church teachings.) Some historians argue that many heretics have performed an essential function by forcing the church to clarify its position.

Martin Luther himself was declared a heretic by the pope in 1521, when he would not recant his teachings, but he survived under the protection of a friendly prince. While heretics are no longer treated in this way, it is nevertheless good to be prepared.

❶ Avoid public heresy.
Heresy is any formal public statement that disagrees with the church on an issue of dogma. The Protestant Reformation emerged from such statements. Martin Luther's Ninety-five Theses, for example, were heretical and entered as evidence at the Diet of Worms in 1521.

Here's what to do if you are accused of heresy:

- Demand an immediate public trial. By this point, your rights may have evaporated. Speak up anyway.*

- State your position clearly and repeatedly. Get it on the record in your own words.

---

* *Although some of this section is written with tongue firmly planted in cheek, The United Methodist Church does indeed have clear and serious procedures for clergy or laypersons charged with "dissemination of doctrine contrary to the established standards of doctrine of The United Methodist Church." There are ways to defend yourself! For details, check out* The Book of Discipline of The United Methodist Church *for the section labeled "Chargeable Offenses and the Statute of Limitations." In the meanwhile, make sure no one in the room has matches.*

If accused of heresy, demand an immediate public trial. State your position clearly.

- Consider your options. If in a church trial you believe you might change enough minds to ward off execution, consider proceeding.

- Support your case with Holy Scripture. In a trial, you will be doomed without sufficient evidence from the Bible, history, and church doctrine.

- If the above steps fail, consider recanting. You could be wrong.

❷ Avoid practicing witchcraft.
Witchcraft is considered a form of heresy, since it depends upon powers other than God and the authority of the church. Practicing witchcraft does *not* include wearing Halloween costumes or reading books about wizards.

❸ Avoid getting nabbed in a political uprising.
Historically, persons who posed a political threat were sometimes burned at the stake. Or crucified. Or not elected.

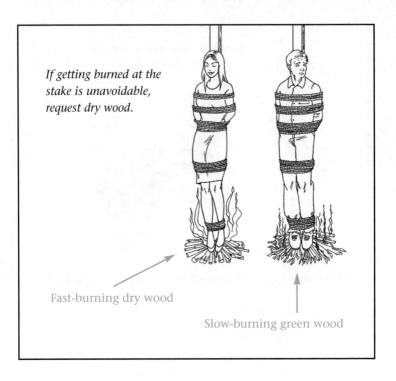

If getting burned at the stake is unavoidable, request dry wood.

Fast-burning dry wood

Slow-burning green wood

Be Aware

- If you find yourself in a situation where being burned at the stake poses an imminent threat, try wearing flame-retardant material.

- If there is no hope of escape, request dry wood and plenty of dry kindling. Green wood burns slower, smokier, and at lower temperatures, causing a more painful and less efficient death.

WORLD RELIGIONS

Listed by approximate number of adherents:

Christianity	2 billion
Islam	1.3 billion
Hinduism	900 million
Agnostic/Atheist/Non-Religious	850 million
Buddhism	360 million
Confucianism and Chinese traditional	225 million
Primal-indigenous	150 million
Shinto	108 million
African traditional	95 million
Sikhism	23 million
Juche	19 million
Judaism	14 million
Spiritism	14 million
Baha'i	7 million
Jainism	4 million
Cao Dai	3 million
Tenrikyo	2.4 million
Neo-Paganism	1 million
Unitarian-Universalism	800,000
Rastafarianism	700,000
Scientology	600,000
Zoroastrianism	150,000

COMPARATIVE RELIGIONS

	Baha'i	Buddhism	Christianity
Founder and date founded	Bahá'u'lláh (1817-1892) founded Babism in 1844 from which Baha'i grew.	Founded by Siddhartha Gautama (the Buddha) in Nepal in the 6th-5th centuries B.C.	Founded on Jesus of Nazareth, a Palestinian Jew, in the early 1st century A.D.
Number of adherents in 2000	About 7 million worldwide; 750,000 U.S.	360 million worldwide; 2 million U.S.	About 2 billion worldwide; 160 million U.S.
Main tenets	The oneness of God, the oneness of humanity, and the common foundation of all religion. Also, equality of men and women, universal education, world peace, and a world federal government.	Meditation and the practice of virtuous and moral behavior can lead to Nirvana, the state of enlightenment. Before that, one is subjected to repeated lifetimes, based on behavior.	Jesus is the Son of God and God in human form. In his death and resurrection, he redeems humanity from sin and gives believers eternal life. His teachings frame the godly life for his followers.
Sacred or primary writing	Bahá'u'lláh's teachings, along with those of the Bab, are collected and published.	The Buddha's teachings and wisdom are collected and published.	The Bible is a collection of Jewish and Near Eastern writings spanning some 1,400 years.

Confucianism	Hinduism	Islam	Judaism
Founded by the Chinese philosopher Confucius in the 6th-5th centuries B.C. One of several traditional Chinese religions.	Developed in the 2nd century B.C. from indigenous religions in India, and later combined with other religions, such as Vaishnavism.	Founded by the prophet Muhammad ca. A.D. 610. The word *Islam* is Arabic for "submission to God."	Shaped by Abraham, Isaac, and Jacob ca. 2000 B.C.
6 million worldwide (does not include other traditional Chinese beliefs); U.S. uncertain.	900 million worldwide; 950,000 U.S.	1.3 billion worldwide; 5.6 million U.S.	14 million worldwide; 5.5 million U.S.
Confucius's followers wrote down his sayings or *Analects*. They stress relationships between individuals, families, and society based on proper behavior and sympathy.	Hinduism is based on a broad system of sects. The goal is release from repeated reincarnation through yoga, adherence to the Vedic scriptures, and devotion to a personal guru.	Followers worship Allah through the Five Pillars. Muslims who die believing in God, and that Muhammad is God's messenger, will enter Paradise.	Judaism holds the belief in a monotheistic God, whose Word is revealed in the Hebrew Bible, especially the Torah. Jews await the coming of a messiah to restore creation.
Confucius's *Analects* are collected and still published.	The Hindu scriptures and Vedic texts.	The Koran is a collection of Muhammad's writings dictated by God.	The Hebrew scriptures compose the Christian Old Testament.

FAMILY TREE OF CHRISTIANITY

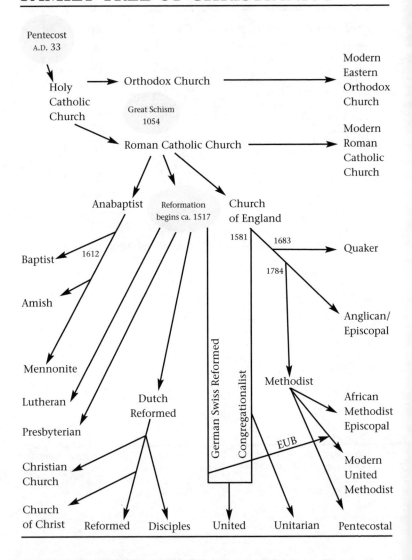

U.S. CHRISTIAN DENOMINATIONS

Listed by approximate number of adult adherents:

Catholic	60 million
Baptist	30 million
Wesleyan (including United Methodists)	13 million
Lutheran	9 million
Pentecostal/Charismatic	5 million
Orthodox	4 million
Presbyterian	4 million
Episcopalian/Anglican	3 million
Churches of Christ	3 million
Congregational/ United Church of Christ	2 million
Assemblies of God	1 million
Anabaptist	600,000
Adventist	100,000

COMPARATIVE DENOMINATIONS:

	Catholic	Orthodox	Lutheran
Founded when and by whom?	Catholics consider Jesus' disciple Peter (died ca. A.D. 66) the first pope. Through Gregory the Great (540-604), papacy is firmly established.	A.D 330: Emperor Constantine renames Byzantium "Constantinople" and declares Christianity the empire's religion.	1517: Martin Luther challenges Catholic teachings with his Ninety-five Theses. 1530: the Augsburg Confession is published.
Adherents in 2000	About 1 billion worldwide; 60 million U.S.	About 225 million worldwide; about 4 million U.S.	About 60 million worldwide; about 9 million U.S.
How is Scripture viewed?	The canon is 46 books in the OT (Apocrypha included) and 27 in the NT. Interpretation is subject to church tradition.	49 OT books (Catholic plus three more) and 27 NT. Scripture is subject to tradition.	Protestant canon contains 39 OT books, 27 NT. Scripture alone is the authoritative witness to the gospel.
How are we saved?	God infuses the gift of faith in the baptized, which is maintained by good works and receiving Penance and the Eucharist.	God became human so humans could be deified, that is, have the energy of God's life in them.	We are saved by grace when God grants righteousness through faith alone. Good works inevitably result, but they are not the basis of salvation.
What is the church?	The mystical body of Christ, who established it with the pope as its head; he pronounces doctrine infallibly.	The body of Christ in unbroken historical connection with the apostles; the Roman pope is one of many patriarchs who govern.	The congregation of believers, mixed with the lost, in which the gospel is preached and the sacraments are administered.
What about the sacraments?	Catholics hold seven sacraments. Baptism removes original sin; usually infants. The Eucharist undergoes transubstantiation.	Baptism initiates God's life in the baptized; adults and children. In the Eucharist, bread & wine are changed into body & blood.	Baptism is necessary for salvation. The Lord's Supper is bread & wine that with God's Word are truly Jesus' body & blood.

Liturgical Churches

	Anglican	Presbyterian	United Methodist
Founded when and by whom?	1534: Henry VIII is declared head of the Church of England. 1549: Thomas Cranmer produces the first *Book of Common Prayer*.	1536: John Calvin writes *Institutes of the Christian Religion*. 1789: Presbyterian Church U.S.A. is organized.	1738: Anglican ministers John and Charles Wesley seek renewal. 1784: U.S. Methodists form a separate church body, 1968 United Methodist.
Adherents in 2000	45-75 million worldwide; about 3 million U.S.	40-48 million worldwide; 4 million U.S.	20-40 million worldwide; about 13 million U.S.
How is Scripture viewed?	Protestant canon accepted. Scripture is interpreted in light of tradition and reason.	Protestant canon accepted. Scripture is "witness without parallel" to Christ, but in human words reflecting beliefs of the time.	Protestant canon accepted. Scripture is primary source for Christian doctrine.
How are we saved?	We share in Christ's victory, who died for our sins, freeing us through baptism to become living members of the church.	We are saved by grace alone. Good works result, but are not the basis of salvation.	We are saved by grace alone. Good works must result, but do not obtain salvation.
What is the church?	The body of Christ is based on "apostolic succession" of bishops, going back to the apostles. In the U.S., it is the Episcopal Church.	The body of Christ includes all of God's chosen and is represented by the visible church. Governed by regional "presbyteries" of elders.	The body of Christ, represented by church institutions. Bishops oversee regions and appoint pastors, who are itinerant.
What about the sacraments?	Baptism brings infant and convert initiates into the church; in Communion, Christ's body & blood are truly present.	Baptism is not necessary for salvation. The Lord's Supper is Christ's body & blood, which are spiritually present to believers.	Baptism is a sign of regeneration; in the Lord's Supper, Jesus is really present.

COMPARATIVE DENOMINATIONS:

	Anabaptist	Congregational	Baptist
Founded when and by whom?	1523: Protestants in Zurich, Switzerland, begin believers' baptism. 1537: Menno Simons begins Mennonite movement.	1607: Members of England's illegal "house church" exiled. 1620: Congregationalists arrive in the New World on the *Mayflower*.	1612: John Smythe and other Puritans form the first Baptist church. 1639: The first Baptist church in America is established.
Adherents in 2000	About 2 million worldwide; about 600,000 U.S.	More than 2 million worldwide; about 2 million U.S.	100 million worldwide; about 30 million U.S.
How is Scripture viewed?	Protestant canon accepted. Scripture is inspired but not infallible. Jesus is living Word; Scripture is written Word.	Protestant canon accepted. Bible is the authoritative witness to the Word of God.	Protestant canon accepted. Scripture is inspired and without error; the sole rule of faith.
How are we saved?	Salvation is a personal experience. Through faith in Jesus, we become at peace with God, moving us to follow Jesus' example by being peacemakers.	God promises forgiveness and grace to save "from sin and aimlessness" all who trust him, who accept his call to serve the whole human family.	Salvation is offered freely to all who accept Jesus as Saviour. There is no salvation apart from personal faith in Christ.
What is the church?	The body of Christ, the assembly and society of believers. No one system of government is recognized.	The people of God living as Jesus' disciples. Each local church is self-governing and chooses its own ministers.	The body of Christ; the redeemed throughout history. The term *church* usually refers to local congregations, which are autonomous.
What about the sacraments?	Baptism is for believers only. The Lord's Supper is a memorial of his death.	Congregations may practice infant baptism or believers' baptism or both. Sacraments are symbols.	Baptism is immersion of believers, only as a symbol. The Lord's Supper is symbolic.

Non-Liturgical Churches

	Churches of Christ	Adventist	Pentecostal
Founded when and by whom?	1801: Barton Stone holds Cane Ridge Revival in Kentucky. 1832: Stone's Christians unite with Disciples of Christ.	1844: William Miller's prediction of Christ's return that year failed. 1863: Seventh-Day Adventist Church is organized.	1901: Kansas college students speak in tongues. 1906: Azusa Street revival in L.A. launches movement. 1914: Assemblies of God organized.
Adherents in 2000	5-6 million worldwide; about 3 million U.S.	About 11 million worldwide; about 100,000 U.S.	About 500 million worldwide; about 5 million U.S.
How is Scripture viewed?	Protestant canon accepted. Scripture is the Word of God. Disciples of Christ view it as a witness to Christ, but fallible.	Protestant canon accepted. Scripture is inspired and without error; Ellen G. White, an early leader, was a prophet.	Protestant canon accepted. Scripture is inspired and without error. Some leaders are considered prophets.
How are we saved?	We must hear the gospel, repent, confess Christ, and be baptized. Disciples of Christ: God saves people by grace.	We repent by believing in Christ as Example (in his life) and Substitute (by his death). Those who are found right with God will be saved.	We are saved by God's grace through Jesus, resulting in our being born again in the Spirit, as evidenced by a life of holiness.
What is the church?	The assembly of those who have responded rightly to the gospel; it must be called only by the name of Christ.	Includes all who believe in Christ. The last days are a time of apostasy, when a remnant keeps God's commandments faithfully.	The body of Christ, in which the Holy Spirit dwells; the agency for bringing the gospel of salvation to the whole world.
What about the sacraments?	Baptism is the immersion of believers only, as the initial act of obedience to the gospel. The Lord's Supper is a symbolic memorial.	Baptism is the immersion of believers only. Baptism and the Lord's Supper are symbolic only.	Baptism is immersion of believers only. A further "baptism in the Holy Spirit" is offered. Lord's Supper is symbolic.

THE SEASONS OF THE CHURCH YEAR AND WHAT THEY MEAN

Advent is a season of longing and anticipation, during which we prepare for the coming of Jesus. The church year begins with Advent, as life begins with birth, starting four Sundays before Christmas. The liturgical color for Advent is blue, which symbolizes waiting and hope, or purple, which signifies royalty (and penitence).

Christmas is a day *and* a season when we celebrate God's coming among us as a human child: Jesus, Emmanuel (which means "God with us"). The liturgical color for Christmas is white, which reminds us that Jesus is the Light of the world. Christmas lasts for 12 days, from December 25 to January 5.

Epiphany is celebrated on January 6, when we remember the three Wise Men's visit to the Christ child. The color for Epiphany Day is white. During the time after Epiphany we hear stories about Jesus' baptism and early ministry. The color for these Sundays is sometimes white and sometimes green. On the last Sunday we celebrate the Transfiguration. The color for this day is white, and we hear the story of Jesus shining brightly on the mountaintop.

Lent is a season when we turn toward God and think about how our lives need to change. This is also a time to remember our baptism, and how that gift gives us a new start every day! The color for Lent is purple, symbolizing repentance. Lent begins on Ash Wednesday and lasts for 40 days (not including Sundays) and ends on the Saturday before Easter Sunday.

The Three Days are the most important part of the Christian calendar because they mark Jesus' last days, death, and resurrection. These days (approximately three 24-hour periods) begin on Maundy Thursday evening and conclude on Easter evening. On *Maundy Thursday* we hear the story of Jesus' last meal with his disciples and his act of service and love in washing their feet. On *Good Friday* we hear of Jesus' trial, crucifixion, death, and burial. On *Saturday* some United Methodist congregations at the nighttime *Easter Vigil* hear stories about the amazing things God has done. It is a night of light, Scripture readings, baptismal remembrance, and Communion. On *Easter Sunday* we celebrate Jesus' resurrection and our new lives in Christ. Easter falls on a different date each year—sometime between March 22 and April 25.

Easter is not just one day, but a whole season when we celebrate the resurrected Jesus. The season begins on Easter Sunday and lasts for 50 days (including Sundays). The color is white, symbolizing resurrection and joy. The Day of Pentecost falls on the 50th day of the season (*Pentecost* means 50th), when we honor the Holy Spirit and the church's mission in the world. This day uses the fiery color of red.

Time after Pentecost is the longest season in the church calendar, lasting almost half the year. Sometimes this is called "ordinary time" because the Sundays are counted with ordinal numbers (fourth, tenth, sixteenth Sunday after Pentecost, etc.). The liturgical color for the time after Pentecost is green, representing life and growth. Each week we hear a different story about Jesus' ministry from one of the four Gospels.

Special festivals are celebrated throughout the year. Some festivals occur the same time every year, such as Reformation Sunday (last Sunday in October) and All Saints Sunday (first Sunday in November). Many congregations recognize public holidays such as Mother's Day and Thanksgiving. United Methodists also have denominational days of remembrance, such as Aldersgate Day, Peace with Justice Sunday, World Communion Sunday, Laity Sunday, United Methodist Student Day, Martin Luther King Jr. Day, and Native American Awareness Sunday.

THE SEASONS
OF THE CHURCH YEAR

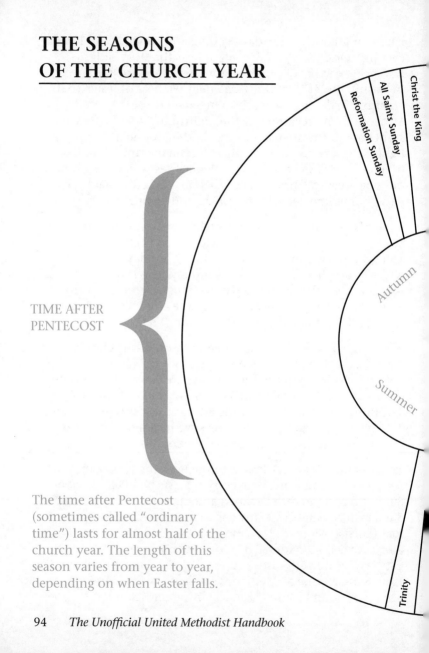

Christ the King

All Saints Sunday

Reformation Sunday

Autumn

Summer

Trinity

TIME AFTER
PENTECOST

The time after Pentecost
(sometimes called "ordinary
time") lasts for almost half of the
church year. The length of this
season varies from year to year,
depending on when Easter falls.

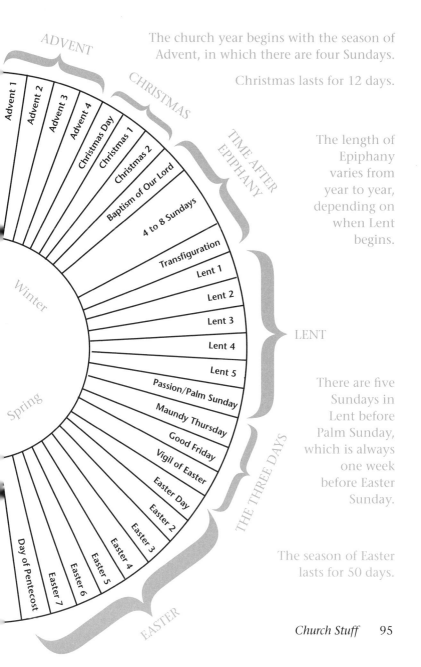

The church year begins with the season of Advent, in which there are four Sundays.

Christmas lasts for 12 days.

The length of Epiphany varies from year to year, depending on when Lent begins.

There are five Sundays in Lent before Palm Sunday, which is always one week before Easter Sunday.

The season of Easter lasts for 50 days.

ADVENT

CHRISTMAS

TIME AFTER EPIPHANY

LENT

THE THREE DAYS

EASTER

Advent 1
Advent 2
Advent 3
Advent 4
Christmas Day
Christmas 1
Christmas 2
Baptism of Our Lord
4 to 8 Sundays
Transfiguration
Lent 1
Lent 2
Lent 3
Lent 4
Lent 5
Passion/Palm Sunday
Maundy Thursday
Good Friday
Vigil of Easter
Easter Day
Easter 2
Easter 3
Easter 4
Easter 5
Easter 6
Easter 7
Day of Pentecost

Winter

Spring

EVERYDAY STUFF

Believing in God involves more than going to church and reading the Bible. It's about keeping your faith with you in every part of your life.

This section includes:

- Advice for helping people in times of trouble.
- Tips on forgiving others and treating them with respect—even if you don't always feel like it.
- Suggestions for avoiding temptation on a daily basis. Some of these ideas go back to the Middle Ages.

HOW TO SHARE YOUR FAITH WITH SOMEONE

Sharing the gospel with others is a natural part of exercising a mature faith. In fact, Jesus commanded his followers to do this, making it an important part of the life of faith (Matthew 28:18-20). Still, many United Methodists tend to be rather shy evangelists.

While *evangelism* has become a negative word for some people, sharing the story of salvation in Jesus Christ is still the most rewarding way to live out one's faith. It is also a discipline that takes practice.

1 Look for the opening.
Regular daily conversations offer lots of chances to talk about your faith. Listen for open-ended comments, such as, "I wonder why life is like that," or, "Sometimes life seems so hard." When possible, offer a response from a Christian perspective. Begin sentences with phrases such as, "I've come to think . . . " or, "I don't have the perfect answer, but I believe . . . "

2 Be yourself.
Expressing your faith should be natural and the same as other types of daily conversation. Avoid suddenly switching your tone of voice or vocabulary. Also, don't try to impress the other person with your knowledge. Allow the Holy Spirit to guide you.

3 Watch for a chance to take the conversation deeper.
Carefully gauge the other person's response. Observe his or her facial expression, verbal tone, and body language. If he or she seems to be closing down, set the topic aside and wait for another time. If he or she keys in and perks up, be prepared to continue.

④ Open up.

Human beings are attracted to each other by our strengths, but we bond because of our weaknesses. Key to sharing your faith is the willingness to be honest about your own life's struggles. This will communicate safety, which for many people is critical.

⑤ Follow up.

Offer to continue the conversation later and arrange a time. At this point, the conversation will have become personally valuable to you. Allowing the person to see your commitment to your faith alongside your continuing questions will reassure him or her of your sincerity.

⑥ Offer to share your faith community with the other person.

Most people join a church after being invited by a friend. When the time is right, invite the person to attend with you. Tell the person what makes it special to you.

⑦ Try to maintain the relationship regardless of what the person does.

Be prepared for the other person to shut down around faith talk, decline your invitation to attend church, or even appear to avoid you. The most effective way to communicate that you're a follower of Jesus Christ is through your actions; continue to live naturally and with integrity. Watch for another opportunity to open the subject later on.

⑧ Celebrate when the Good News becomes good news for someone.

When someone comes to faith or grows in the faith (either because of or in spite of your witness), find a way to share that joy. Stay in touch with the new believer.

HOW TO PRAY

Prayer is intimate communication with God and can be used before a meal, at bedtime, during a worship service, or any time the need or opportunity arises. Silent and spoken prayers are both okay and may be used liberally throughout the day. Prayer is also taking time to listen to what God is saying to us. You can use the great historic prayers of the church. (For example, look at pages 876–879 and prayers 890–896 in *The United Methodist Hymnal*. In fact, many of the hymns can help you form words for praying.) Save prayers from church bulletins or websites. There is a special strength that comes from knowing that saints before us have prayed in these words. Spontaneous prayer is sometimes best, and the following process may help build the habit.

❶ Assess your need for prayer.
Take stock of the situation at hand, including your motivations. What are you praying *for* and why?

❷ Select a type of prayer.
Prayers of *supplication* (requests for God's help), *contrition* (in which sin is confessed and forgiveness requested), *intercession* (on behalf of others), and others are good and time tested. Prayers can be lament ("Have you forgotten me, Lord?"), thanksgiving ("I am grateful for your gift, O God"), and submission ("Not my will, but Yours").

❸ Select a physical prayer posture.
Many postures are appropriate:

- A most common type of prayer in the New Testament is from a prone position, lying face-down on the ground, arms spread.

- Kneeling with your face and palms upturned is good for prayers of supplication.

- Seated, bowed head with closed eyes and hands folded is common today and aids concentration.

- Prayer can be offered with eyes wide open, for example, perhaps when looking at the person for whom you are praying, or (please!) when you are praying as you drive!

Choose a comfortable and appropriate prayer posture for your prayer time.

④ Offer your prayer.
Pray with confidence. God listens to all prayer and responds. Breathe deeply, relax, and be open as the Spirit leads you.

⑤ Listen.
Take time during your prayer simply to listen. Some prayer traditions involve only silent meditation as a means of listening for God's voice.

HOW TO WORK FOR PEACE AND JUSTICE ON BEHALF OF PEOPLE WHO ARE POOR AND OPPRESSED

Knowing that good works are the result—not the cause—of salvation, United Methodists have a long and extraordinary record of working for economic justice and relief around the world. United Methodist Committee on Relief, for example, ranks among the world's most powerful aid organizations, often responding faster, longer, and with larger resources than other groups.

❶ Include people who are poor and oppressed in your daily prayers.

Keeping the needs of others in mind, especially people who suffer as a result of economic inequality, political oppression, or natural disaster, defines a person's good works. Name specific situations in your prayers and use specific place names and people's names whenever possible. Keep the newspaper on your lap as you pray, if necessary.

❷ Include people who are poor and oppressed in your personal or household budget.

Dedicate some of your personal giving to economic-aid organizations. This should include your congregation. If you already tithe (give 10 percent of your income to your church), consider offering what United Methodist often call "second mile giving," offerings designated for relief agencies and specialized ministries over all of the world. (In United Methodist jargon, this kind of giving is called "Advance Specials.")

❸ Pay close attention to economic and political conditions in other nations.

You can't help if you don't know what's really going on. Resolve to be a well-informed person who tests the worldview in the news against the worldview in the Bible. Utilize the Internet to locate independent and alternative news sources with unique, on-the-spot perspectives.

❹ Get to know organizations that work for justice locally.

Your congregation probably already organizes to do justice work in your neighborhood. If not, consider taking responsibility to organize a ministry team in your church.

❺ Make working for justice part of your weekly or monthly routine.

Devote a portion of your time regularly to a specific activity that personally connects you to people who are poor and disenfranchised. There is no substitute for personal contact. John Wesley even called it "a means of grace."

❻ Vote your conscience.

If you are of voting age, remember that nations will be judged by the way they treat people who are disadvantaged. Keep this in mind when you go to your polling place.

❼ Advocate for a cause in which you believe, one that has meaning for you personally.

HOW TO IDENTIFY A GENUINE MIRACLE

The term *miracle* describes something that causes wonder. It is usually used in reference to an event that defies logical explanation and appears to be the work of a higher force, suggesting a reality beyond the five senses.

1 Disregard most minor situations.
The facts should indicate a situation of high order, such as one that is life threatening, one involving suffering, or involving an immediate threat. Finding your lost keys may be pleasant but does not necessarily constitute a miracle.

2 Look for a lack of predictability.
A positive outcome should be needed and wanted, but not expected. Miracles tend to occur "out of the blue" rather than as the result of an earthly cause, especially a human one.

3 Evaluate the outcome.
Miracles achieve a life-giving purpose; they never occur outside the will of God. Suffering is relieved, God is glorified, Jesus' presence is made manifest, the lowly are lifted up, evil is thwarted, creation is revealed, or life is saved. The outcome *must* be regarded as good, according to biblical standards.

❹ Look for a divine agency.

The ability to make a miracle happen, to guarantee the results, or to take credit for it is beyond human. Often, the event will defy what we know to be true about the laws of nature or probability. If anyone stands to make money or advance an agenda from an event, it is most likely not a miracle.

❺ Adopt a wait-and-see perspective.

A miracle will still be a miracle later on. Labeling something a miracle too quickly could lead down unhelpful paths, while waiting to make the call—pondering the event in your heart—will enhance your faith journey.

Be Aware

- The most overlooked miracle is that God shows up in everyday life events and in such ordinary forms as bread, juice, water, words, and people.

- The miracle of life in Jesus Christ is a daily event and should be regarded as a free gift.

THREE ESSENTIAL PERSONAL SPIRITUAL RITUALS

A spiritual ritual is a routine for building one's faith. Ritual involves action, words, and often images that work together to center one's daily life in Jesus Christ. Medical studies show that people who pray regularly throughout the day suffer less stress, have lower incidence of heart disease, and live longer on average than those who do not.

❶ Morning Devotions

- Directly upon awakening, turn your attention first to God. The silence and solitude available in the morning hours are ideal.

- Try to make prayer the first activity of your day. If necessary, set your alarm to sound 15 minutes early to give yourself time.

- Begin with thanks and by remembering God's constant presence.

- Identify events you anticipate in your day and how you feel about them.

- Ask God to provide what you need for the day.

- Pray on behalf of other people. Consider keeping a list of names tucked inside your Bible or devotional book.

❷ Mealtime Grace

Human beings naturally pause before a meal. Use those moments to give thanks.

- Consider establishing mealtime grace as a household ritual.

- When eating in public, be considerate of others, but do not abandon your ritual.

- Once your meal is assembled and ready to eat, take time before praying to gather your thoughts and call an appropriate prayer to mind.

Praying before mealtime is a great personal ritual that can be shared with others.

- Many people pray a rote or memorized prayer at mealtimes. Consider occasionally departing from your regular prayer with an extemporaneous one.

❸ Evening Prayer

The other daily rituals you perform in the evening, like brushing your teeth or letting the cat out, create a natural structure for evening prayer.

- Establish a regular time, such as sunset or bedtime, and commit to it.

- Confess wrongdoing and ask for forgiveness.

- Tell God about the joys and sorrows of the day. Ask for help with the sorrows and give thanks for the joys.

- Identify the good things about the day. On bad days, find at least one thing to give thanks for.

- Consider using a devotional as a guide and companion.

- Think about involving other members of your household in this ritual. Evening prayer particularly can be enhanced through sharing. When children are included, consider tracing the cross on their foreheads and say a brief blessing as part of the ritual. When appropriate, remind a child of his or her baptism. Who was present? Which pastor baptized the child? How did the child respond? What did the congregation do? Did the child scream so loudly that the pastor seemed relieved to "toss the kid back to the parents"?

HOW TO CONFESS YOUR SINS AND RECEIVE FORGIVENESS

Confession is an "office of the keys" (see Matthew 16:19) belonging to all baptized persons, that is, anyone may confess and any believer may pronounce the word of forgiveness. A declaration of forgiveness is permanent and binding because it comes from Jesus Christ himself.

1 Make a mental list of your offenses.

2 Locate a fellow Christian.
When appropriate, confess your sins to another person.

3 Resolve to confess of your own free will.
Don't confess merely because someone else wants you to do it. Make your confession voluntarily.

4 Make your confession fearlessly, aloud if possible.
Confess the sins that burden you, and then confess the sins of which you are not aware or can't remember.

5 Avoid making up sins.
More important than the facts and figures is a spirit of repentance in your heart. Sad to say, but our human competitive desire may tempt us even to confess that "my sins are juicier than your sins." Even the apostle Paul claimed to be "the chief of sinners." Most of us have enough sin to confess without having to make up stuff! Thinking "I am worse than anyone one else" is only the other side of the "I'm better than anyone else" coin.

6 Receive forgiveness as it is given, in the name of the Father and of the Son and of the Holy Spirit.
God forgives you fully. Carry a small eraser in your pocket or purse as a reminder that you have been

forgiven. Some persons make the sign of the cross to help them remember that forgiveness comes from God.

7 Resolve to live joyfully and penitently.
With absolution comes new life in the freedom of God's grace.

Be Aware

- Unburdening your conscience through confession is cleansing and good for the soul; it's not meant to be torture.

- Ultimately, forgiveness comes from God. A perfect and pure confession is not a strict requirement to receive it.

HOW TO FORGIVE SOMEONE

Forgiving is one of the most difficult disciplines of faith, since it seems to cost you something additional when you've already been wronged. Swallowing your pride and seeking a greater good, however, can yield great healing and growth for all concerned.

1 Acknowledge that God forgives you.
When you realize that God has already shown forgiveness, and continues to forgive sinners like you, it's easier to forgive someone else.

2 Consult Scripture.
Jesus taught the Lord's Prayer to his disciples, who were hungry to become like him. Forgiveness was a big part of this. Read Matthew 6:9-15.

3 Seek the person out whenever possible.
Consciously decide to deliver your forgiveness in person. In cases where this is geographically impossible, find an appropriate alternative means, such as the telephone.

Note: This may not be wise in all cases, given the timing of the situation or the level of hurt. Certain problems can be made worse by an unwelcome declaration of forgiveness. Consult with a clergyperson before taking questionable action.

4 Say, "I forgive you," out loud.
A verbal declaration of forgiveness is ideal. Speaking the words enacts a physical chain reaction that can create healing for both speaker and hearer. In the Bible, Jesus used these words to heal a paralyzed man from across a room.

⑤ Pray for the power to forgive.
Praying for this is always good, whether a forgiveness situation is at hand or not. It is especially helpful in cases where declaring forgiveness seems beyond your reach.

Be Aware

- When people sin against you personally, forgiving them does NOT depend upon their feeling sorry (showing contrition) or asking for your forgiveness. But it helps. You may have to struggle, however, to forgive them without their consent or participation.

- If your effort to forgive is rejected, pray that your spirit will continue to be forgiving. There is no spiritual gift in the nagging pursuit of someone who does not want forgiveness or who thinks no forgiveness is necessary or who simply wants nothing else to do with you.

- At minimum, live out the forgiveness you wish to offer, even if you do not feel ready to say it aloud.

- To fail to forgive someone who has wronged you, even after he or she has died, is to allow that person to continue to control your life. Rather, let God's Spirit control you!

HOW TO DEFEND YOUR FAITH AGAINST ATTACK

Defending your faith from attack involves tact and savvy, that is, the ability to empathize with your adversary and use his or her affronts creatively without getting baited into an angry or hostile response. (The United Methodist theological perspective was hammered out in a context of debate and controversy, particularly in eighteenth-century England.) Just be ready. There is no substitute for knowing your stuff.

❶ Employ the 80/20 rule.
In any debate, it is best to listen at least 80 percent of the time and talk 20 percent of the time.

❷ Engage in empathic listening.
Empathic listening means to try to comprehend not just the content of the other person's position, but also the emotional thrust behind it. This is important especially in cases where the speaker's emotional expressions are intense.

❸ Restate your adversary's argument empathetically.
Use sentences like, "So, you're upset because Christians seem to say one thing and do another."

❹ Identify with what the speaker is saying.
For example, say, "I know what you mean. I see a lot of phony behavior at my own church." This elevates the conversation and keeps it civil.

❺ Do your best to put the speaker at ease.
Having made clear that you understand his or her position, you are free to state your defense or counterpoint. Offer "I statement" responses, such as, "I wonder

how I would stand up under that kind of scrutiny, myself," or, "I do my best not to judge others too harshly. I'd hate to be judged by those standards."

❻ Keep it as upbeat as possible.
Use humility, humor, and a pleasant nature to defuse any tension. In this context, humor would not include such statements as "You have a good point; if you parted your hair differently, everyone could see it" or "Keep repeating: 'Socks first, then shoes.'"

❼ Give your opponent his or her due.
When the speaker makes a good argument, say, "You make a good point." This will further elevate the conversation. If you still disagree, make your counter-argument calmly.

❽ Avoid closing off the conversation or leaving it on a sour note.
If you can, offer to continue the discussion over a lunch that you buy. Avoid falling into a "winner take all" mind-set. Keep respect as your highest value.

Be Aware

- Attacks on faith are not limited to verbal assaults, especially in countries such as China or Vietnam, where religious persecution is a reality. Take care when visiting such places, especially when distributing religious materials or sharing stories about your faith.

- It is best in all cases to avoid sounding smug or preachy where your points resemble counterattacks.

- You don't need to defend God. God can handle criticism. You are supporting your own faith experience. (United Methodists like the word "experience.")

HOW TO RESIST TEMPTATION

Folks who like to stay up late at night reading the dictionary report that the word "tempt" has roots which are shared with the Latin word "tendere," which means "to stretch." Temptation does that—stretching us sometimes to the point of breaking. Martin Luther gave some advice about resisting temptation and United Methodists don't hesitate to borrow good advice!

❶ **Run the opposite direction.**
Learn to identify the things that tempt you and avoid situations in which temptation will occur. When you see a temptation coming down the road, take a detour.

❷ **Laugh at the tempter.**
Temptations are simply things that want to gain power over you. When you laugh at them, you reduce them to their proper place.

❸ **Distract yourself with other, healthier activities.**
God knows what's good for you and so do you. Find an alternate activity that promotes trust in God and requires you to care for your neighbors. Seek the company of others, especially people to whom you may be of service.

❹ **Remember, your Lord also confronted temptation.**
Jesus faced down temptation by telling the devil the truth, namely, only God is Lord. Consider using a contemporary version of Jesus' words: "God's in charge here, not you."

Be Aware

• There are different kinds of temptation. Regardless of the type, temptation always involves a hidden voice whispering to you, "No matter what God says, you really

Even Jesus faced temptation when the devil confronted him in the wilderness.

need to trust me instead. I'm the only thing that can help you."

- Temptations try to make us trust in ourselves or in other things more than in God. When you realize this, you'll see that everything on the list above is just turning back to Jesus who died to show you how much you can trust him.

- Temptation is like false advertising. By all appearances the sin to which you are being tempted is attractive, something desirable, and a bargain. Only after you have bought the product do you see it for what it is: destructive, at worst, and in need of repair, at best.

HOW TO CARE FOR THE SICK

While a trained and licensed physician must be sought to treat illness and injury, there is no malady that cannot be helped with faithful attention and prayer.

❶ Assess the nature of the problem.
Visit a local pharmacy if the illness is a simple one. Over-the-counter medications usually provide temporary relief until the body heals itself. If symptoms persist, the sick person should see a doctor and get a more detailed diagnosis.

❷ Pray for them.
Intercessory prayers are prayers made on someone else's behalf. Recent studies point to healing in hospitalized patients who have been prayed for—even when the sick were not aware of the prayers. Add the afflicted person to your church's prayer list.

❸ Call in support.
Prayer and emotional support from friends and family are vital parts of healing, living with illness, and facing death. Ask the pastor to assemble the church leaders for prayer and the laying on of hands.

Here's what the Bible says on this topic: "Are any among you sick? They should call for the elders of the church and have them pray over them, anointing them with oil in the name of the Lord" (James 5:14).

Be Aware

- Many people claim expertise in healing, from acupuncturists and herbalists to "faith healers" and psychics. Use caution and skepticism, but keep an open mind.

- Many people believe that much healing can be found in "comfort foods," such as homemade chicken soup.

- Many United Methodist congregations have <u>trained laypeople called Stephen Ministers.</u> They are prepared to have "one with one" caring relationships with persons who are sick (or troubled in other ways).

- Those who attempt to diagnose and treat their own symptoms can often do more harm than good. When in doubt, always consult a pharmacist, doctor, or other medical professional.

Gather friends, family, and church leaders to pray and lay hands on sick people.

HOW TO IDENTIFY AND AVOID EVIL

The devil delights in unnoticed evil. To this end, the devil employs a wide array of lies, disguises, and deceptions while attacking our relationships with God and each other.

❶ Know your enemy.
Evil appears in many forms, most often using camouflage to present itself as kindly or friendly. Cruelty, hatred, violence, and exploitation are among the many forms evil can take, but it often masquerades as justice or something done "for their own good." Be alert to acts, people, and events that employ these methods, even if the eventual outcome appears good.

❷ Proceed carefully and deliberately.
Avoid rushing to conclusions. Use good judgment.

❸ Take action to expose the evil.
Evil relies on darkness. It hates the light of truth. Things that fear public knowledge or scrutiny might be evil.

❹ Be prepared to make a personal sacrifice.
Fighting evil can be costly. A successful counterattack may require you to give up something you cherish. For Jesus, as for many of his followers, it was his life. Love is the foundation of sacrifice that combats evil.

❺ Stay vigilant.
Evil's genius is shown in disguise, deception, and misdirection. Maintain your objectivity and apply the biblical measures of right and wrong you know to be correct. John Wesley said a good conscience was an evidence of the prevenient grace of God.

HOW TO AVOID GOSSIP

Gossip is among the most corrosive forces within a community and should be monitored closely. Discovery of gossip should be viewed as an opportunity to defend your neighbors' integrity, both gossiper and gossipee. It has been said that an expert gossiper is someone who can turn an earful into a mouthful. "I don't repeat gossip, so listen carefully the first time."

1 **Determine whether the conversation at hand qualifies as gossip.**

- Gossip involves one party speaking about a second party to a third party.

- The person who is the topic of gossip is not a participant in the conversation.

- The tone of the conversation is often secretive or negative. Gasps and whispers are common.

- The facts expressed in a gossip conversation are often unsubstantiated and have been obtained second- or third-hand.

2 **Recall and heed Titus 3:2: "Speak evil of no one."**

3 **Interject yourself into the conversation politely.**
Ask whether the gossiper(s) have spoken directly to the person about whom they are talking. If not, politely ask why. This may give some indication why they are gossiping.

4 **Make a statement of fact.**
Gossip withers in the face of truth. Make an attempt to parse out what is truly known from conjecture and

Avoid gossip. It undermines community and damages relationships.

supposition. State aloud that gossip is disrespectful and unfair.

⑤ Offer an alternative explanation based on fact. Describe other situations that cast the gossipee in a favorable light. Always try to give people the benefit of the doubt.

Be Aware

• There is a fine line between helping and meddling. Pay close attention to your own motivations and the possible outcomes of your actions.

• Gossip injures both the gossiper and the person who is the subject of rumors.

• Consult the Eighth Commandment (see Exodus 20:16).

• For further help, consult James 4:11.

HOW TO RESOLVE INTERPERSONAL CONFLICT

Disagreements are part of life. They often occur when we forget that not everyone sees things the same way. Conflict should be viewed as an opportunity to grow, not a contest for domination. Resolution of interpersonal conflict is not enhanced by an attitude which says, "Well, you go your way and I'll go (piously cast eyes heavenward) *His*!"

❶ Adopt a healthy attitude.
Your frame of mind is critical. Approach the situation with forethought and calm. Prayer can be invaluable at this stage. Do not approach the other party when you're angry or upset.

❷ Read Matthew 18:15-20 beforehand.
Consult the Bible to orient your thinking. This is the model Jesus provided and can be used to call to mind an appropriate method.

❸ Talk directly to the person involved.
Avoid "triangulation." Talking about someone to a third party can make the conflict worse, as the person may feel that he or she is the subject of gossip.

❹ Express yourself without attacking.
Using "I statements" can avoid casting the other person as the "bad guy" and inflaming the conflict. "I statements" are sentences beginning with phrases such as "I feel . . . " or "I'm uncomfortable when . . . "

❺ Keep "speaking the truth in love" (Ephesians 4:15) as your goal.
Your "truth" may not be the other party's. Your objective

is to discover and honor each other's "truth," not to put down the other person.

⑥ Seek out a third party to act as an impartial witness. If direct conversation doesn't resolve the conflict, locate someone both parties trust to sit in. This can help clarify your positions and bring understanding.

⑦ Build toward forgiveness and a renewed friendship. Agree upon how you will communicate to prevent future misunderstandings.

Be Aware

- Seemingly unrelated events in your or the other person's life may be playing an invisible role in the conflict at hand. Be ready to shift the focus to the real cause.

- You may not be able to resolve the conflict at this time, but don't give up on future opportunities.

- For seemingly intractable disagreements, The United Methodist Church offers the resources of JUSTPEACE, a mission of the church that strives for justice, reconciliation, and preservation and restoration of community.

When two people aren't getting along, sometimes an impartial third person can help resolve the dispute.

HOW TO CONSOLE SOMEONE

Consolation is a gift from God. Christians in turn give it to others to build up the body of Christ and preserve it in times of trouble. (See 2 Corinthians 1:4-7.) United Methodists often employ food as a helpful secondary means. (Brownies seem particularly effective . . . as does apple pie . . . or . . .)

1 Listen first.
Make it known that you're present and available. When the person opens up, be quiet and attentive.

2 Be ready to help the person face grief and sadness, not avoid them.
The object is to help the person name, understand, and work through these feelings, not gloss over them.

3 Avoid saying things to make yourself feel better.
"I know exactly how you feel" is seldom true and trivializes the sufferer's pain. Even if you have experienced something similar, no experience is exactly the same. If there is nothing to say, simply be present.

4 Show respect with honesty.
Don't try to answer the mysteries of the universe or force your beliefs on the person. Be clear about the limitations of your abilities. Be ready to let some questions go unanswered. <u>Consolation isn't about having all the answers, it's about bearing one another's burdens.</u>

5 Don't put words in God's mouth.
Avoid saying, "This is God's will" or "This is part of God's plan."

Be Aware
- Your pastor or a Stephen Minister (See "How to Care for the Sick") could be your consultant for unusual situations.

HOW TO COPE
WITH LOSS AND GRIEF

Some Christians tend to downplay their losses by saying, "Well, it could be worse." This may provide only temporary relief at best. Any loss can cause pain, feelings of confusion, and uncertainty. These responses are normal.

① Familiarize yourself with the stages of grief.
Experts identify five: denial, anger, bargaining, depression, and acceptance. Some add hope as a sixth stage. Grieving persons cycle back and forth among the stages, sometimes experiencing two or three in a single day. This is normal.

② Express your grief.
Healthy ways may include crying, staring into space for extended periods, ruminating, shouting at the ceiling, and sudden napping. Laughing outbursts have been known to happen and should not be judged harshly.

③ Identify someone you trust to talk to.
Available people can include a spouse, parents, relatives, friends, a pastor, a doctor, or a trained counselor. Many household pets also make good listeners and willing confidants.

④ Choose a personal way to memorialize the loss.
Make a collage of photographs, offer a memorial donation to your church, or start a scrapbook of memories to honor the event. This helps you to begin to heal without getting stuck in your grief.

Be Aware
• Grief occurs with many kinds of losses: death, separation, radical change in life circumstance, job demotion,

shift in friendship, and, for some people, defeat in the league championship basketball game when a three-point shot falls for the sinister opposing team with two seconds left in the game.

- Many experts prescribe a self-giving activity, such as volunteering at a shelter or soup kitchen, as a means of facilitating a healthy grieving process.

- The pain immediately after suffering a loss is usually deep and intense. This will lessen with the passage of time.

- Anger, guilt, bitterness, and sadness are likely emotions.

- Short-term depression may occur in extreme cases. After experiencing a great loss, such as the death of a loved one, make an appointment with your family physician for a physical.

- Even Jesus cried when his friend Lazarus died (John 11:35).

Even Jesus felt the loss of Lazarus when he died.

Mary   Martha

THE TOP TEN ATTRIBUTES TO LOOK FOR IN A SPOUSE

While no single personality trait can predict a compatible marriage, the following list frames some basic things to look for in a spouse. With all attributes, some differences can be the source of a couple's strength rather than a source of difficulty. Statistically, United Methodists appear to be about as successful at choosing a spouse as other people.

❶ Similar values.
Values that concern religious beliefs, life purpose, financial priorities, and children are a foundation on which to build the relationship. Contrary values tend to create discord.

❷ Physical-energy and physical-space compatibility.
Consider whether the person's energy level and physical-space needs work with yours. Also, the word *compatibility* can mean a complementary match of opposites, or it can denote a match based on strong similarities.

❸ Physical and romantic compatibility.
If the two of you have a similar degree of interest in or need for physical and romantic expression in your relationship, the chance of lifelong compatibility increases.

❹ Intellectual parity.
Communicating with someone who has a significantly different intelligence level or educational background can require extra effort.

5 Emotional maturity.

A lifelong relationship of mutual challenge and support often helps each person grow emotionally, but a lifetime spent waiting for someone to grow up could be more frustration than it's worth.

6 Sense of humor.

Sense of humor can provide an excellent measure of a person's personality and an important means to couple survival. If he or she doesn't get your jokes, you could be asking for trouble. Or perhaps you need to get new (and better) jokes. Here is a quick test: do you find this amusing? *A Freudian slip is when you mean one thing and say a mother.* If you liked that, you might want to hear about the man who went to Norway and made a fjordian slip. Or you might not.

7 Respect.

Look for someone who listens to you without trying to control you. Look also for a healthy sense of self-respect.

8 Trustworthiness.

Seek out someone who is honest and acts with your best interests in mind—not only his or hers—and tries to learn from his or her mistakes.

9 Forgiving.

When you sincerely apologize to your spouse, he or she should try to work through and get beyond the problem rather than hold on to it. Once forgiven, past mistakes should not be raised, especially in conflict situations.

10 Kindness.

An attitude of consistent kindness may be the most critical attribute for a lifelong partnership.

Be Aware

- If you live to be old, you will probably experience major changes that you cannot predict at age 15 or 25 or 35. Accepting this fact in advance can help you weather difficult times.

- Use all of your resources—intuition, emotions, and rational thought—to make the decision about a life partner.

- Family members and trusted friends can offer invaluable advice in this decision-making process and should be consulted.

- United Methodists might, on the other hand, draw some caution from the way that Charles Wesley broke up a relationship between his brother John and Grace Murray. History suggests that John was right about Grace Murray and Charles was wrong.

- Growth in a relationship is a sign of its health. Christian Newcomer, an early United Brethren leader, was not very romantic in describing his choice of a mate: "I had to seek a housekeeper, which I found in Miss Elizabeth Baer." They were married for 39 years and the warmth of their love grew and was expressed when at the death of his wife Newcomer wrote, "My dear companion departed this life . . . (she was) a staff and comfort unto me; soon we shall be reunited where parting shall be no more."

- The advice of one nineteenth-century circuit rider to those preachers who were looking for a wife was: Marry a woman who has a good disposition before she gets religion, so that if she loses her religion, you are none the worse off.

- There ain't no explainin' love.

HOW TO BANISH THE DEVIL FROM YOUR PRESENCE

Since God loved the flesh so much as to redeem it by becoming flesh (John 1:14), Protestants often believe that the devil, by contrast, hates the flesh. Bodily acts, therefore, hold the power to send the devil packing. While the existence of a "personal" devil—a physical entity embodying pure evil—has a part in some Christian tradition, United Methodists tend to withhold final judgment on specifics. Still, it's good to be prepared.

1 Laugh out loud.
Laughter is abhorrent to the devil and should be indulged in frequently. You can practice now. *Do you know the difference between how pastors count attendance and how ushers count attendance? Ushers count noses; pastors count nostrils.*

2 Look at a cross or make the sign of the cross.
The devil hates the cross because that is where God's love for you is most evident.

3 Seek the company of other believers.
Play games with children, attend worship, join a prayer team, host a dinner party, or locate a Bible study. Solitude can provide the devil an opportunity.

4 Serve those who have less than you.
Resolve to volunteer your time to help those less fortunate than you. The devil is thwarted by the love of Christ in action.

5 Confess your sins.
The devil is attracted to a guilty conscience. Confession clears the conscience and emboldens the believer.

6 Break wind.

The devil (along with anyone else in the room) might well leave you alone. (This was one of Martin Luther's favorites. You may want to ask Dr. Luther about this when you get to heaven.)

7 Consider what you might be doing to invite the devil into your life.

We invite the devil into our lives when our actions and values no longer center on Christ.

Banish the devil by taking part in activities with others.
Avoid excessive solitude.

HOW TO BE SAVED (BY GRACE THROUGH FAITH AND NOT BY YOUR GOOD WORKS)

Some religions are built on the idea that the more closely people follow the religious rules or the more morally people behave, the better God will like them—and the better God likes them, the greater their chances of "getting into heaven."

Christianity, on the other hand, says that out of pure love God was willing to sacrifice everything—even his only Son—to save you forever from sin, death, and all your false gods. Including you.

Since God has already done everything needed to secure your salvation through Jesus, you never have to do one single thing to earn God's favor. United Methodists understand that good works are the inevitable harvest of salvation through faith but are not the way to salvation. In fact, the Wesleys and Otterbein all saw such significance to the growth after pardon for sin that they challenged believers to move on to Perfection, perfect love of God and of neighbor. In a sense, salvation is completed (perhaps appropriated is a better word) by the loving works that follow (and give evidence of) the gift of faith. Jacob Albright wrote, "Real joy, genuine happiness, occur only through the consciousness of duties fully performed." Even those good works (holy living, sanctification) come as a gift of grace. Grace saves; faithful living follows.

❶ Get familiar with the word "grace."
Grace means that God gives you all the good stuff—forgiveness, salvation, love, and life, with all its ups and

downs—as totally free gifts. Keep an eye out for situations in which you can use this word, and then use it liberally. You'll soon begin to see God's grace all around you.

❷ Practice letting go of things you love.

Staying focused on yourself can make it difficult to open up to a grace-filled world. But giving of yourself, your time, and your possessions can put you in a receptive, open frame of mind. This is important, as salvation cannot be "found" by looking for it, it is only revealed.

❸ Lose yourself as often as possible.

An important part of having a receptive frame of mind is losing yourself in whatever you're doing. To do this, give yourself over entirely to the activity. This can be accomplished in prayer and worship, but also through things like playing games, talking with friends and family, reading a good book, serving others, or playing a musical instrument. Even work can accomplish this.

❹ Admit your limitations.

Without straying into despair or false modesty, make an honest confession to yourself about what you can and cannot do, what you are and what you are not. When you see yourself realistically you become more open to God's message of love, grace, and salvation.

❺ Accept your uniqueness.

In God's eyes, you were so valuable as to merit the ultimate sacrifice of his Son, even before you spoke your first words. God will spend your whole life trying to convince you of this. When you accept that to God you are priceless beyond imagining it becomes easier to understand why God chose to save you.

6 Spend time in worship and prayer to the living God.
While only God grants the faith that saves, the church
gives lots of opportunities where God has promised to
come to you.

7 Put "doing" into perspective.
The "old Adam" or "old Eve" in you—the sinner in
you—always wants to be in charge over God. He or she
will tell you that God's grace is too good to be true and
that you must "do" something to earn or justify it.
Simply remind him or her that you were baptized into
Jesus Christ and have all the grace you need. Then the
good you do is not to earn grace but because of it, joyful
acts of obedience to the one who has already loved you.

Be Aware

- The apostle Paul's summary of the gospel goes like this:
  "For by grace you have been saved through faith, and
  this is not your own doing; it is the gift of God—not the
  result of works, so that no one may boast" (Ephesians
  2:8-9).

- All of the branches that form the United Methodist tree
  have taught that each individual is invited to accept
  God's gift of grace. (This contrasts with a view that says
  that God chooses some to be saved—and perhaps some
  to be damned.) Because of free will, a person can say no
  to the gift. Not only that, but it is possible to fall from
  grace, possible to turn away from grace once accepted.

- Charles Wesley wrote a hymn claiming the free gift of
  God's grace for all who will accept it ("Come, Sinners, to
  the Gospel Feast").

HOW TO REFORM THE CHURCH WHEN IT STRAYS FROM THE GOSPEL

When Martin Luther nailed his Ninety-five Theses to the church door in 1517, he took a stand against the corruption he saw in the church—false gospels, immoral leaders, and bad theology—and launched the Reformation.

When John Wesley saw the Church of England move away from the biblical visions of evangelism and a sacramental life, he helped to shape the Methodist movement as an effort to recapture New Testament power.

When Jacob Albright felt that the tradition of his birth no longer had the expectation that faith would express itself in holy living, he gathered others who sought to let Christ make a difference in their daily lives. Out of this emerged The Evangelical Association.

When Philip William Otterbein began to fear the lack of discipline and spiritual maturity among followers of Christ, he drew up a covenant for all (male) believers to sign, including submitting themselves to church discipline.

To stay faithful to the gospel, the church still depends on all its members to call it back, not to their own personal visions, but to Jesus' vision.

❶ Know your stuff.
You can't call the church back to the gospel if you don't learn for yourself what the gospel is. Read your Bible regularly. Also, spend time in conversation with good theologians, like pastors and church leaders. But remember that you, too, are a theologian!

② Trust your conscience, but equip it first with good information.

To challenge church authorities, Wesley, Albright, and Otterbein had to draw strength from even more powerful sources, namely faith in God and conscience. "It is neither safe nor right," Luther said, "to go against conscience." Wesley claimed that conscience could be the work of God's grace (even among non-believers).

③ Double-check and triple-check your motivations. Are you fighting on behalf of the gospel or for your own personal agenda?

Knowing the difference between the two matters. Some things may be worthy social causes that deserve your time and attention, but they may not be the gospel.

④ Speak out. Act.

It isn't enough just to take a stand or hold an opinion. Once you're sure you're doing it for the right reasons, find an effective way to make change happen.

Luther nailed the Ninety-five Theses in a public place (a common way to speak to the public in his day) and later used the printing press to spread his opinions to the widest possible audience. He put himself in the line of fire.

John Wesley wrote treatises and pamphlets and books to spread the renewal of the church. Letters to the editor in London papers became a place for Wesley to exchange ideas with those who disagreed with him.

⑤ Prepare to defend yourself, and your message of reform, from attack.

People tend to dislike reform—and institutions like it even less. While the church calls us to model the love of Christ and live by his teachings, sometimes the church and its leaders respond to reformers with a "kill the messenger" attitude.

⑥ Keep steady, be patient, and listen to wise counsel. Reformation can take decades to take root. Renewal leaders debate with each other about the best way to bring the gospel to a new age and restore the church to its real purpose.

Be Aware

- Just because "everybody" agrees with you does not mean you are right.
- Just because the church "has always done it that way" does not mean it is wrong.
- God is a living God. Could God be saying something new to the church?

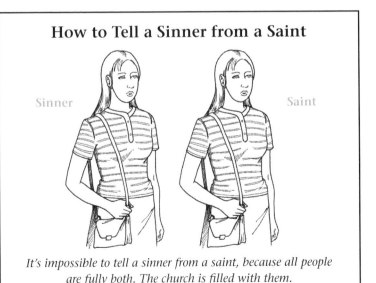

How to Tell a Sinner from a Saint

Sinner　　　　　　　　　　　　　　Saint

It's impossible to tell a sinner from a saint, because all people are fully both. The church is filled with them.

HOW TO ENCOUNTER THE HOLY TRINITY AS ONE GOD IN THREE PERSONS

The Trinity is a mystery. Even great theologians don't completely understand, and some scholars spend their whole lives studying it. After 2,000 years, Christians still believe in this mystery because it gives life and shape to everything in our lives—our relationships, our faith, and especially our worship.

1 Get to know these Trinitarian creeds: the Nicene Creed (No. 880 in *The United Methodist Hymnal*) and the Apostles' Creed (Nos. 881 and 882 in *The United Methodist Hymnal*).

These "symbols," as they are sometimes called, were written during different times of crisis when heresies threatened the church's unity and clear statements about what Christians believed were needed. While different from each other, they each teach a lot about the three-personed God.

2 Include the baptismal words as a regular part of your prayer life and worship life.

"In the name of the Father, and of the Son, and of the Holy Spirit" was spoken at your baptism. If you make a sign of the cross, you trace a physical reminder of the Trinity on your body. (Making the sign of the cross seems strange to some United Methodists, but others find it a powerful reminder.)

3 Understand that you were made in God's image.

Just as the one God is Father, Son, and Holy Spirit all at once, you are mind, body, and soul all at once. Because you reflect the image of God, you were made

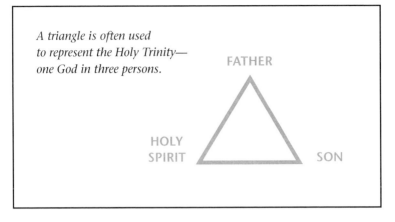

A triangle is often used to represent the Holy Trinity— one God in three persons.

FATHER

HOLY
SPIRIT

SON

to live a life of worship in which everything you do and say honors God.

❹ Spend time in the community of faith.
Go to worship, fellowship, Bible study, Sunday School, and anything else that regularly keeps you in the company of other Christians.

❺ Seek out God's Word and the means of grace.
The Trinity is revealed in reading the Bible, preaching, the Sacraments, the forgiveness of sins, the community of believers, and within anything else where Jesus, the living Word, is active.

Be Aware

• Some people use handy metaphors to try to get a handle on the doctrine of the Trinity. For example, water takes three major forms: liquid, solid, and gas. Yet it remains one substance. Such metaphors are very useful to a point, but ultimately they must give way to the divine mystery that remains. All human figures of speech fall short of the divine mystery.

HOW TO BECOME A THEOLOGIAN OF THE CROSS (AND AVOID BEING A THEOLOGIAN OF GLORY)

The term *theologian* technically means a student of or specialist in theology. And *theology* is the study of God and God's relationship with humanity and the universe. You may not consider yourself a specialist yet, but you definitely are a student of theology. As a theologian, you take note of some issues that continue to tempt Christians away from central gospel truth. This twenty-first century generation is not the first to struggle with whether or not God gives secular success to those with faith. One way to state this question is "theology of cross or theology of glory."

❶ Position the cross in your thinking as an end point, not a starting point.
The cross of Jesus Christ is the most important and powerful thing in Christian faith. But it's easy to misunderstand what this means. A "theologian of glory," based on nothing more than individual wishes, tries to use the cross as a starting point for personal gain—to make people healthy and wealthy, successful and popular. A "theologian of the cross," in contrast, thinks of the cross as the last stop for sin, death, and delusions of grandeur. In other words, the cross is an end point.

❷ Determine to become a theologian of the cross.
The apostle Paul explains this approach: "For I decided to know nothing among you except Jesus Christ and him crucified" (1 Corinthians 2).

❸ Identify the marks of the theology of glory and practice contrasting them with the theology of the cross.

A theologian of glory might say something like: "Accept Jesus as your personal Lord and Savior and he will make you happier, richer, and better looking." If things don't pan out, the theologian of glory will say that you need to have greater faith, believe more, or try harder.

A theologian of the cross, on the other hand, emphasizes what Jesus did for us. In baptism, Jesus gives you his word, which essentially says, "You are mine," even when you feel troubled, poor, or unattractive.

❹ Look for God to be revealed in the most unexpected places.

A theologian of glory thinks that God shows up where humans expect God to show up: in things that are powerful, wise, and important by human standards. On the other hand, the theologian of the cross knows that God is much subtler: God shows up in those things that seem weak, foolish, and insignificant to human eyes. (See 1 Corinthians 1:17-29.)

❺ Accept the lifelong nature of becoming a theologian of the cross.

In the end, being a theologian of the cross is something that can't be taught from a book. There's no class you can take or diploma you can get that certifies you as a theologian of the cross. As you experience life's ups and downs, being a theologian of the cross is something you just live into when you are open and trust God's promises.

BIBLE STUFF

Written down by many people over hundreds of years, the Bible is more like a portable bookshelf than one book by itself. And because the Bible is God's Word, people often feel overwhelmed when they try to read it.

This section includes:

- Helpful information about when, where, and why people wrote the 66 books within the Bible. (It didn't all come together at once.)
- Tips for reading and understanding the Bible— how it's organized and what it says.
- Some of the most mystifying, hair-raising, and just plain off-the-wall stories in the Bible.

COMMON TRANSLATIONS OF THE BIBLE

Translation	Grade Level*	Theological Affiliation	Year Released	Special Features
King James Version	12.0	Church of England, conservative and evangelical	1611	Poetic style using Elizabethan English. Most widely used translation for centuries.
New American Standard Bible	11.0	Conservative and evangelical	1971; updated, 1995	Revision of the 1901 American Standard Version into contemporary language.
New Revised Standard Version	8.1	Mainline and interconfessional	1989	Updated version of the Revised Standard Version.
New King James Version	8.0	Transnational, transdenominational, conservative, and evangelical	1982	Updates the King James text into contemporary language.
New International Version	7.8	Transnational, transdenominational, conservative, and evangelical	1978; revised, 1984	Popular modern-language version. Attempts to balance literal and dynamic translation methods.
Today's English Version (also called the Good News Bible)	7.3	Evangelical and interconfessional	1976	Noted for its freshness of language.

	Grade level*	Theological tradition	Date	Description
New American Bible	6.6	Roman Catholic	1970; revised NT, 1986; revised Psalms, 1991	Official translation of the Roman Catholic Church in the United States.
New Living Translation	6.4	Evangelical	1996	A meaning-for-meaning translation. Successor to the Living Bible.
New Century Version	5.6	Conservative and evangelical	1988; revised, 1991	Follows the *Living Word Vocabulary*.
Contemporary English Version	5.4	Conservative, evangelical, mainline	1995	Easy-to-read English for new Bible readers.
The Message	4.8, from NT samples	Evangelical	2002	An expressive paraphrase of the Bible.

*The grade level on which the text is written, using Dale-chall, Fry, Raygor, and Spache Formulas.

Bible classifications

Apocrypha Bible: Contains certain books that most Protestants don't consider Scripture. Most of these OT books are accepted by the Roman Catholic Church.

Children's Bible: Includes illustrations and other study aids that are especially helpful for children.

Concordance Bible: Lists places in the Bible where key words are found.

Red Letter Bible: The words spoken by Christ appear in red.

Reference Bible: Pages include references to other Bible passages on the same subject.

Self-Proclaiming Bible: Diacritical marks (as in a dictionary) appear above difficult names and words to help with the pronunciation.

Text Bible: Contains text without footnotes or column references. May include maps, illustrations, and other helpful material.

61 ESSENTIAL BIBLE STORIES

	Story	Bible Text	Key Verse
1.	Creation	Genesis 1-2	Genesis 1:27
2.	The Human Condition	Genesis 3-4	Genesis 3:5
3.	The Flood and the First Covenant	Genesis 6-9	Genesis 9:8
4.	The Tower of Babel and Abraham and Sarah	Genesis 11-12	Genesis 12:1
5.	Sarah, Hagar, and Abraham	Genesis 12-25	Genesis 17:19
6.	Isaac and Rebecca	Genesis 22-25	Genesis 24:67
7.	Jacob and Esau	Genesis 25-36	Genesis 28:15
8.	Joseph and God's Hidden Ways	Genesis 37-50	Genesis 50:20
9.	Moses and Pharaoh	Exodus 1-15	Exodus 2:23
10.	The Ten Commandments	Exodus 20	Exodus 20:2
11.	From the Wilderness into the Promised Land	Exodus 16-18; Deuteronomy 1-6; Joshua 1-3, 24	Deuteronomy 6:4
12.	Judges	Book of Judges	Judges 21:25
13.	Ruth	Book of Ruth	Ruth 4:14
14.	Samuel and Saul	1 Samuel 1-11	1 Samuel 3:1
15.	King David	multiple OT books	1 Samuel 8:6
16.	David, Nathan, and What Is a Prophet?	2 Samuel 11-12	2 Samuel 7:12
17.	Solomon	1 Kings 1-11	1 Kings 6:12
18.	Split of the Kingdom	1 Kings 11ff	1 Kings 12:16
19.	Northern Kingdom, Its Prophets and Fate	1 Kings—2 Kings 17	Amos 5:21
20.	Southern Kingdom, Its Prophets and Fate (Part 1)	multiple OT books	Isaiah 5:7

61 ESSENTIAL BIBLE STORIES

	Story	Bible Text	Key Verse
21.	Southern Kingdom, Its Prophets and Fate (Part 2)	multiple OT books	Jeremiah 31:31
22.	The Exile	Isaiah 40-55; Ezekiel	Isaiah 40:10
23.	Return from Exile	multiple OT books	Ezra 1:1
24.	Ezra and Nehemiah	Books of Ezra and Nehemiah	Ezra 3:10
25.	Esther	Book of Esther	Esther 4:14
26.	Job	Book of Job	Job 1:1
27.	Daniel	Book of Daniel	Daniel 3:17
28.	Psalms of Praise and Trust	Psalms 8, 30, 100, 113, 121	Psalm 121:1
29.	Psalms for Help	various psalms	Psalm 22:1
30.	Wisdom	Job, Proverbs, Ecclesiastes	Proverbs 1:7
31.	The Annunciation	Luke 1:26-56	Luke 1:31-33
32.	Magi	Matthew 2:1-12	Matthew 2:2-3
33.	Birth of Jesus	Luke 2:1-20	Luke 2:10-11
34.	Simeon	Luke 2:25-35	Luke 2:30-32
35.	Wilderness Temptations	Matthew 4:1-11; Mark 1:12-13; Luke 4:1-13	Luke 4:12-13
36.	Jesus' Nazareth Sermon	Matthew 13:54-58; Mark 6:1-6: Luke 4:16-30	Luke 4:18-19, 21
37.	Jesus Calls the First Disciples	Matthew 4:18-22; Mark 1:16-20; Luke 5:1-11	Luke 5:9-10
38.	Beatitudes	Matthew 5:3-12	Luke 6:20-26
39.	Gerasene Demoniac	Matthew 8:28-34; Mark 5:1-20; Luke 8:26-39	Luke 8:39
40.	Feeding of the 5,000	Matthew 14:13-21; Mark 6:30-44; Luke 9:10-17; John 6:1-14	Luke 9:16-17

61 ESSENTIAL BIBLE STORIES

	Story	Bible Text	Key Verse
41.	The Transfiguration	Matthew 17:1-8; Mark 9:2-8: Luke 9:28-36	Luke 9:34-35
42.	Sending of the Seventy	Matthew 8:19-22; Luke 10:1-16	Luke 10:8, 16
43.	Good Samaritan	Luke 10:25-37	Luke 10:27-28
44.	Healing the Bent-Over Woman	Luke 13:10-17	Luke 13:16
45.	Parables of Lost and Found	Luke 15:1-32	Luke 15:31-32
46.	Rich Man and Lazarus	Luke 16:19-31	Luke 16:29-31
47.	Zacchaeus	Luke 19:1-11	Luke 19:9
48.	Sheep and Goats	Matthew 25:31-46	Matthew 25:40
49.	Parable of the Vineyard	Matthew 21:33-46; Mark 12:1-12; Luke 20:9-19; (Isaiah 5:1-7)	Luke 20:14-16
50.	The Last Supper	Matthew 26:20-29; Mark 14:12-16: Luke 22:14-38	Luke 22:19-20, 27
51.	Crucifixion	Matthew 27; Mark 15; Luke 23; John 19	Luke 23:42-43, 46
52.	Road to Emmaus	Luke 24	Luke 24:30-31
53.	Pentecost	Acts 2:1-21	Acts 2:17-18
54.	Healing the Lame Man	Acts 3-4	Acts 4:19
55.	Baptism of the Ethiopian	Acts 8:26-39	Acts 8:35-37
56.	Call of Saul	Acts 7:58—8:1, 9:1-30	Acts 9:15-16
57.	Peter and Cornelius	Acts 10	Acts 10:34-35
58.	Philippians' Humility	Philippians 2:1-13	Philippians 2:12-13
59.	Love Hymn	1 Corinthians 13	1 Corinthians 13:4-7
60.	Resurrection	1 Corinthians 15	1 Corinthians 15:51-55
61.	Final Reign	Revelation 21-22	Revelation 21-1

HOW TO READ THE BIBLE

The Bible is a collection of 66 separate books gathered together over hundreds of years and thousands of miles. Divided into the Old Testament (Hebrew language) and the New Testament (Greek language), these writings have many authors and take many forms.

The Bible includes histories, stories, prophecies, poetry, letters, songs, teachings, and laws, to name a few. Christians believe the Bible is the story of God's relationship with humankind and a powerful way that God speaks to people.

❶ Determine your purpose for reading.
Clarify in your own mind what you hope to gain. Your motivations should be well intentioned, such as to seek information, to gain a deeper understanding of God and yourself, or to enrich your faith. Pray for insight before every reading time.

❷ Resolve to read daily.
Commit to a daily regimen of Bible reading. Make it a part of your routine until it becomes an unbreakable habit.

Commit to reading the Bible daily.

❸ Master the mechanics.

• Memorize the books of the Bible in order.

chapter number

↓

Proverbs 26:11

↗   ↑

book name   verse number

• Familiarize yourself with the introductory material. Many Bible translations include helpful information at the front of the Bible and at the beginning of each book.

• The books are broken down into chapters and verses. Locate the beginning of a book by using the Bible's table of contents. Follow the numerical chapter numbers; these are usually in large type. Verses are likewise numbered in order within each chapter. Simply run your finger down the page until you locate the verse number you're looking for.

• If your Bible contains maps (usually in the back), consult them when cities, mountains, or seas are mentioned in your reading.

❹ Befriend the written text.
Read with a pen or pencil in hand and underline passages of interest. Look up unfamiliar words in a dictionary. Write notes in the margins when necessary. The Bible was written to be read and used, not worshiped.

❺ Practice reading from the Bible out loud.

Be Aware

- Some contemporary versions do not indicate chapters and verses. (The chapter and verses were not part of the original texts.)

- Note whether the Bible you are reading is a translation (word for word from one language to another or meaning for meaning from one language to another) or a paraphrase (seeking to find an easy-to-understand way of saying the same thing as the text means). A paraphrase is likely to reflect the theological bias and perspective of the ones doing the paraphrasing, although translations also force translators to make many decisions, opening the door to interpretation.

- John Wesley said that the Bible was twice inspired, once when written and again when read. Passing attention only to either half of that formula can lead to only half of what God has to say. God was with those who wrote the Scriptures and God will be with you (challenging you, opening new doors for you, bringing fresh learnings to you, comforting you, inspiring you) as you read the Bible today.

- Over 300 years ago, John Wesley explained how he worked with confusing passages in the Bible. (If you have never been confused while reading the Bible, you can skip this section.) Wesley prayed for understanding; then he checked out the difficult passage with parallel texts that were clearer; after further meditation, Wesley would talk with others in the community of faith (a good check and balance!); and then he would read what ancient commentaries had said. He called it "plain truth for plain people" but he knew enough to know that God's will and intent was deep enough to take more than one quick digging.

HOW TO MEMORIZE A BIBLE VERSE

Memorizing Scripture is an ancient faith practice. Its value is often mentioned by people who have, in crisis situations, remembered comforting or reassuring passages coming to mind, sometimes decades after first memorizing them. There are three common methods of memorization.

Method 1: Memorize with Music

Choose a verse that is special for you. It is more difficult to remember something that doesn't make sense to you or that lacks meaning.

1 Choose a familiar tune.
Pick something catchy and repetitious.

2 Add the words from the Bible verse to your tune.
Mix up the words a bit, if necessary. Memorizing a verse "word for word" isn't always as important as learning the message of the verse.

3 Mark the verse in your Bible.
This will help you find it again later on. Consider highlighting or underlining it.

4 Make the words rhyme, if possible.

Method 2: The Three S's
(See it, Say it, Script it)

This method works on the principle of multisensory reinforcement. The brain creates many more neural pathways to a memory through sight, speech, and manipulation (writing) than just one of these, so recall is quicker and easier.

1. Write the verse on index cards in large print. Post the cards in places you regularly look, such as the refrigerator door or bathroom mirror.

2. Say the verse out loud. Repeat the verse ten times to yourself every time you notice one of your index cards.

3. Write the verse down.

4. Try saying and writing the verse at the same time. Repeat.

Write the verse out longhand several dozen times.

Method 3: Old-Fashioned Memorization

Attempt this method only if you consider yourself to be "old school" or if the other methods fail.

1 Write the verse out by hand on paper.
A whiteboard can work extremely well, also. Consider writing it as many as 100 times. Repeat this process until you can recite the verse flawlessly.

2 Don't get up until you've memorized the verse.
Open your Bible to the appropriate verse, sit down in front of it, and don't get up, eat, sleep, or use the bathroom until you can recite it flawlessly.

3 Enlist a family member or friend to help you.
Have them read along with you and prompt you when you get stuck. Do not expect family members to forgo their own meals and routines as you seek to learn by heart Numbers 7:42-59. They might cut you a little slack for 1 Corinthians 13.

THE TOP TEN BIBLE VILLAINS

❶ Satan

The Evil One is known by many names in the Bible and
appears many places, but the devil's purpose is always
the same: To disrupt and confuse people so they turn
from God and seek to become their own gods. This Bible
villain is still active today.

❷ The Serpent

In Eden, the serpent succeeded in tempting Eve to
eat from the tree of the knowledge of good and evil
(Genesis 3:1-7). As a result, sin entered creation.
If it weren't for the serpent, we'd all still be walking
around naked, eating fresh fruit, and living forever.

❸ Pharaoh (probably Seti I or Rameses II)

The notorious Pharaoh from the book of Exodus
enslaved the Israelites. Moses eventually begged him to
"Let my people go," but Pharaoh's heart was hardened
and he refused. Ten nasty plagues later, Pharaoh
relented, but then changed his mind again. In the end,
with his army at the bottom of the sea, Pharaoh finally
gave his slaves up to the wilderness. Perhaps he should
have taught his army how to swim.

❹ Goliath

"The Philistine of Gath," who stood six cubits in height
(about nine feet tall), was sent to fight David, still a
downy-headed youth. Goliath was a fighting champion
known for killing people, but David drilled Goliath
in the head with a rock from his sling and gave God
the glory (1 Samuel 17). The rumor is not true
that Goliath had an early career as a professional
basketball player.

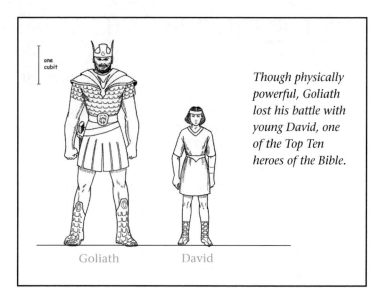

Though physically powerful, Goliath lost his battle with young David, one of the Top Ten heroes of the Bible.

one cubit

Goliath   David

⑤ Jezebel

King Ahab of Judah's wife and a follower of the false god Baal, Jezebel led her husband away from God and tried to kill off the prophets of the Lord. Elijah the prophet, however, was on the scene. He shamed Jezebel's false prophets and killed them (1 Kings 18:40).

⑥ King Herod

Afraid of any potential threat to his power, upon hearing about the birth of the Messiah in Bethlehem Herod sent the Wise Men to pinpoint his location. Awestruck by the Savior in the cradle, the Wise Men went home by a different route and avoided Herod. In a rage, he ordered the murder of every child two years of age or younger in the vicinity of Bethlehem. The baby Messiah escaped with his parents to Egypt (Matthew 2:14-15). The "massacre of the innocents" is not seen on most Christmas cards.

❼ The Pharisees, Sadducees, and Scribes

They dogged Jesus throughout his ministry, alternately challenging his authority and being awed by his power. It was their leadership, with the consent and blessing of the people and the Roman government, that brought Jesus to trial and execution.

❽ Judas

One of Jesus' original disciples, Judas earned 30 pieces of silver by betraying his Lord over to the authorities. He accomplished this by leading the soldiers into the garden of Gethsemane where he revealed Jesus with a kiss (Matthew 26–27). Most scholars deny the suggestion of some that Judas was really a friend trying to help out Jesus.

❾ Pontius Pilate

The consummate politician, the Roman governor chose to preserve his own bloated status by giving the people what they wanted: Jesus' crucifixion. He washed his hands to signify self-absolution, but bloodied them instead.

❿ God's People

They whine, they sin, they turn their backs on God over and over again. When given freedom, they blow it. When preached repentance by God's prophets, they stone them. When offered a Savior, we kill him. In the end, it must be admitted, God's people—us!—don't really shine. Only by God's grace and the gift of faith in Jesus Christ do we have hope.

THE TOP TEN BIBLE HEROES AND HEROINES

The Bible is filled with typical examples of heroism, but another kind of hero and heroine inhabit the pages of the Bible—those people who, against all odds, follow God no matter the outcome. These are champions of faith.

1 Noah

In the face of ridicule from others, Noah trusted God when God chose him to build an ark to save a remnant of humanity from destruction. Noah's trust became part of a covenant with God.

Noah trusted God, even though others made fun of him. By following God's instructions and building a great ark, Noah and his family survived the flood (Genesis 6–10).

❷ Abraham and Sarah

In extreme old age, Abraham and Sarah answered God's call to leave their home and travel to a strange land, where they became the parents of God's people.

❸ Moses

Moses, a man with a speech impediment, challenged the Egyptian powers to deliver God's people from bondage. He led a rebellious and contrary people for 40 years through the wilderness and gave them God's law.

❹ Rahab

A prostitute who helped Israel conquer the promised land, Rahab was the great-grandmother of King David, and thus a part of the family of Jesus himself. (Matthew 1:5)

❺ David

Great King David, the youngest and smallest member of his family, defeated great enemies, turning Israel into a world power. He wrote psalms, led armies, and confessed his sins to the Lord.

❻ Mary and Joseph

These humble peasants responded to God's call to be the earthly parents of the Messiah, although the call came through a pregnancy that was not the result of marriage.

❼ The Canaanite Woman

Desperate for her daughter's health, the Canaanite woman challenged Jesus regarding women and race by claiming God's love for all people (Matthew 15:21-28). Because of this, Jesus praised her faith.

⑧ Peter

Peter was a man quick to speak but slow to think. At Jesus' trial, Peter denied ever having known him. But in the power of forgiveness and through Christ's appointment, Peter became a leader in the early church.

⑨ Saul/Paul

Originally an enemy and persecutor of Christians, Paul experienced a powerful vision of Jesus, converted, and became the greatest missionary the church has ever known.

⑩ Phoebe

A contemporary of Paul's, Phoebe is believed to have delivered the book of Romans after traveling some 800 miles from Cenchrea near Corinth to Rome. A wealthy woman, she used her influence to travel, protect other believers, and to host worship services in her home.

Phoebe is believed to have delivered the book of Romans after traveling 800 miles.

THE THREE MOST REBELLIOUS THINGS JESUS DID

1 The prophet returned to his hometown (Luke 4:14-27).
Jesus returned to Nazareth, where he was raised and was invited to read Scripture and preach. First, he insisted that the scriptures he read were not just comforting promises of a distant future, but that they were about him, local boy, anointed by God. Second, he insisted God would bless foreigners with those same promises through him. These statements amounted to the unpardonable crime of blasphemy!

2 The rebel thumbed his nose at the authorities (John 11:55—12:11).
Jesus had become an outlaw, hunted by the religious authorities who wanted to kill him. Mary, Martha, and Lazarus threw a thank-you party for Jesus in Bethany, right outside Jerusalem, the authorities' stronghold. In spite of the threats to his life, Jesus went to the party. This was not just rebellion but a demonstration of how much Jesus loved his friends.

3 The king rode a royal procession right under Caesar's nose (Matthew 21:1-17; Mark 11:1-10; Luke 19:28-38; John 12:12-19).
Jesus entered Jerusalem during a great festival, in full view of adoring crowds, as a king come home to rule. Riding the colt, heralded by the people with cloaks and branches, accompanied by the royal anthem (Psalm 118), he rode in to claim Jerusalem for God and himself as God's anointed. The Roman overlords and the Jewish leaders watched this seditious act and prepared for a crucifixion.

THE SEVEN FUNNIEST BIBLE STORIES

Humor isn't scarce in the Bible; you just have to look for it. For example, God tells Abraham (100 years old) and Sarah (in her 90s) they'll soon have a son. Understandably, they laugh. Later, they have a son named Isaac, which means "he laughs." Bible humor is also ironic, gross, and sometimes just plain bizarre.

❶ Gideon's dog-men (Judges 6:11—7:23).
God chooses Gideon to lead an army against the Midianites. Gideon gathers an army of 32,000 men, but this is too many. God tells Gideon to make all the men drink from a stream, and then selects only the 300 men who lap water like dogs.

❷ David ambushes Saul in a cave while he's "busy" (1 Samuel 24:2-7).
While pursuing David cross-country to engage him in battle, Saul goes into a cave to "relieve himself" (move his bowels). Unbeknownst to Saul, David and his men are already hiding in the very same cave. While Saul's doing his business, David sneaks up and cuts off a corner of Saul's cloak with a knife. Outside afterward, David shows King Saul the piece of cloth to prove he could have killed him "on the throne."

❸ King David does the goofy (2 Samuel 12-23).
David is so excited about bringing the Ark of the Covenant to Jerusalem that he dances before God and all the people dressed only in a linen ephod, an apron-like garment that covered only the front of his body.

The doomed city of Sodom

Lot's wife ignored God's warning. She looked back at the city of Sodom and became a pillar of salt.

Pillar of salt
(formerly Lot's wife)

❹ Lot's wife (Genesis 19:24-26).
While fleeing God's wrath upon the cities of Sodom and Gomorrah, Lot's wife forgets (or ignores) God's warning not to look back upon the destruction and turns into a woman-sized pillar of salt.

❺ Gerasene demoniac (Mark 5:1-20).
A man is possessed by so many demons that chains cannot hold him. Jesus exorcises the demons and sends them into a herd of 2,000 pigs, which then run over the edge of a cliff and drown in the sea. The herders, now 2,000 pigs poorer, get miffed and ask Jesus to leave.

⑥ Disciples and loaves of bread (Mark 8:14-21).
The disciples were there when Jesus fed 5,000 people with just five loaves of bread and two fish. They also saw him feed 4,000 people with seven loaves. Later, in a boat, the disciples fret to an exasperated Jesus because they have only one loaf for 13 people.

⑦ Peter can't swim (Matthew 14:22-33).
Blundering Peter sees Jesus walking on the water and wants to join him. But when the wind picks up, Peter panics and starts to sink. In Greek, the name Peter means "rock."

Peter, "the rock," sank when he looked to himself instead of to Jesus. Jesus later described Peter as a Rock of the church (Matthew 16:18).

THE FIVE GROSSEST BIBLE STORIES

❶ Eglon and Ehud (Judges 3:12-30).
Before kings reigned over Israel, judges ruled the people. At that time, a very overweight king named Eglon conquered Israel and demanded money. A man named Ehud brought the payment to Eglon while he was perched in his "cool roof chamber" (probably a euphemism meaning "toilet"). Along with the money, Ehud handed over a little something extra—his sword, which he buried so far in Eglon's belly that the sword disappeared into the king's fat and, as the Bible says, "the dirt came out" (v. 22).

❷ Job's sores (Job 2:1-10).
Job lived a righteous life yet he suffered anyway. He had oozing sores from the bald spot on top of his head clear down to the soft spot on the bottom of his foot. Job used a broken piece of pottery to scrape away the pus that leaked from his sores.

❸ The naked prophet (Isaiah 20).
God's prophets went to great lengths to get God's message across to the people. Isaiah was no exception. God's people planned a war, but God gave it the thumbs down. Isaiah marched around Jerusalem naked *for three years* as a sign of what would happen if the people went to war.

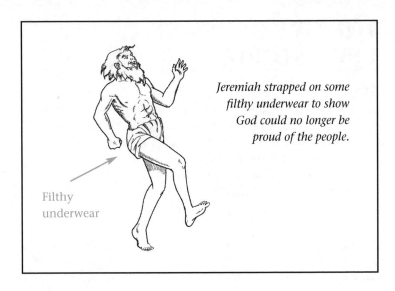

Jeremiah strapped on some filthy underwear to show God could no longer be proud of the people.

Filthy underwear

④ The almost-naked prophet (Jeremiah 13:1-11).
God sent Jeremiah to announce that God could no longer be proud of the people. To make the point, Jeremiah bought a new pair of underclothes, wore them every day without washing them, then buried them in the wet river sand. Later, he dug them up, strapped them on, and shouted that this is what has happened to the people who were God's pride!

⑤ Spilling your guts (Matthew 27:1-8; Acts 1:16-19).
Judas betrayed Jesus and sold him out for 30 pieces of silver. He bought a field with the ill-gotten loot. Guilt-stricken, Judas walked out to the field, his belly swelled up until it burst, and his intestines spilled out on to the ground.

FIVE FACTS ABOUT LIFE
IN OLD TESTAMENT TIMES

① Almost everyone wore sandals.
They were called "sandals" because people walked on sand much of the time.

② There were no newspapers.
People got news by hearing it from other people. Spreading important news was like a giant game of "telephone."

③ It was dark.
Homes, often tents, were typically lit at night by an oil lamp, if at all.

④ You had to fetch your water, which was scarce.
Rich folks had servants to carry it for them, but most people had to carry household water in jugs or leather bags, usually some distance, from a river or well.

⑤ Life expectancy was short.
Despite some long-lived exceptions described in the book of Genesis, such as Abraham (175 years) and Methuselah (969 years), few people lived past 50.

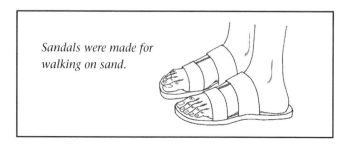

Sandals were made for walking on sand.

TEN IMPORTANT THINGS THAT HAPPENED BETWEEN THE OLD AND NEW TESTAMENTS

The period of time described in the Old Testament ended about 400 years before Jesus' birth. The people of God kept living, believing, struggling, and writing during that period. Here are some of the important events that took place between the Testaments.

1 The Hebrew nation dissolved.
In 587 B.C., the Babylonians destroyed Jerusalem and Solomon's temple, and took the people into exile. Judah was never again an independent kingdom.

2 The people scattered.
After the exile to Babylon ended, the people of Judah moved to many different places. Some of them later came back, but many never did. Some of them lived in Babylon, some lived in Egypt, and some just scattered elsewhere.

3 A religion replaced a nation.
As a result of items 1 and 2, the people's religion changed. They no longer had a state or national religion (Judean religion). Instead, they had a freestanding faith called Judaism.

❹ The Aramaic language became popular.
Because Aramaic was the international language of the
Persian Empire, many Jews quit speaking Hebrew and
spoke Aramaic instead. This is why Jesus spoke Aramaic.

❺ Alexander the Great conquered the world.
Around 330 B.C., Alexander the Great conquered the
Mediterranean and Mesopotamian world. As a result,
Greek became the everyday language of business and
trade in the region. This is why the New Testament was
written in Greek.

❻ The hammer dropped.
Around 170 B.C., the Seleucid emperor outlawed circum-
cision and the Sabbath, and defiled the temple. A family
of Jews called the Maccabees (which means "hammer")
led a revolt.

❼ The Hebrew Scriptures were finished.
During this time, the individual books that make up
what we call the Old Testament were finished. Several
other religious books written at this time (mostly in
Greek) aren't in the Protestant Bible but are part of the
Apocrypha.

**❽ The Sadducees, Pharisees, Essenes, Samaritans,
Zealots, and other groups of people sprouted up.**
Different schools of thought developed within Judaism.
Most of their disagreements were over the idea that
God's people would be resurrected to eternal life.

⑨ God seemed to have forgotten the promise.

God promised King David that one of his descendants would always be king in Jerusalem. But after the Babylonian exile, there were no kings in Jerusalem. People wondered what had happened to God's promise.

⑩ The Roman Empire expanded.

In 63 B.C., the Roman Empire conquered Palestine, having already conquered pretty much everyone else in the region. This is why the Roman Empire ruled the area during the time of Jesus and the New Testament.

FIVE FACTS ABOUT LIFE
IN NEW TESTAMENT TIMES

❶ Synagogues were not always buildings.
For worship, Jesus' people gathered in all kinds of places, often outdoors. "Church" was any gathering of people for worship.

❷ Houses were boxy.
Most houses had a flat roof with an outside staircase leading to it. Inhabitants would sleep on the roof during hot weather. Air conditioning was very rare because the electrical cords had to run all the way to the nineteenth century.

Houses in New Testament times were boxy.

❸ Every town had a marketplace.
Usually there was just one marketplace per town, but one could buy almost everything needed to live.

❹ People ate a lot of fish.
The most common fish in the Sea of Galilee were catfish and carp. Roasting over a charcoal fire was the most common method of cooking.

❺ Dogs were shunned.
The Jewish people in Jesus' day did not keep dogs as pets. Dogs were considered unclean because they ate garbage and animal carcasses.

THE FIVE BIGGEST MISCONCEPTIONS ABOUT THE BIBLE

❶ The Bible was written in a short period of time.
Christians believe that God inspired the Bible writers, the first of whom may have been Moses. God inspired people to write down important histories, traditions, songs, wise sayings, poetry, and prophetic words. All told—from the first recordings of the stories in Genesis to the last decisions about Revelation—the entire Bible formed over a period spanning anywhere from 800 to 1,400 years!

❷ One person wrote the Bible.
Unlike Islam's Koran, which was written down by the prophet Muhammad, the books of the Bible claim the handiwork of many people. Much of Scripture does not identify the human hand that wrote it, so some parts of the Bible may have been written by women as well as men.

❸ The entire Bible should be taken literally.
While many parts of the Bible are meant as descriptions of actual historical events, other parts are intended as *illustrations of God's truth*, such as Song of Solomon, the book of Revelation, and Jesus' parable of the good Samaritan. So when Jesus says, "If your right eye causes you to sin, tear it out and throw it away" (Matthew 5:29), please do not take the saying literally! Scholars doubt that Jesus went around saying "Baa, Baa!" even though the Bible calls him Lamb of God.

❹ People in Bible times were unenlightened.
During the 1,400 years it took to write the Bible, some of history's greatest thinkers lived and worked. Many of these philosophers, architects, mathematicians, orators, theologians, historians, doctors, military tacticians, inventors, engineers, poets, and playwrights are still quoted today and their works are still in use.

❺ The Bible is a single book.
The Bible is actually a collection of books, letters, and other writings—more like a library than a book. There are 39 books in the Hebrew scriptures, what Christians call the "Old" Testament, and 27 books (mostly letters) in the New Testament. There are seven books in the Apocrypha (books written between the Old and New Testaments), or "deuterocanonical" books.

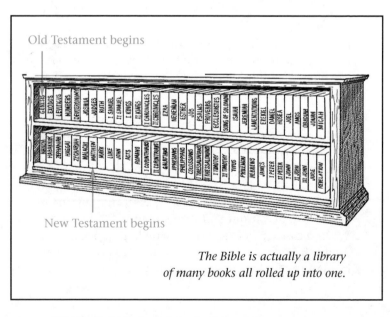

Old Testament begins

New Testament begins

*The Bible is actually a library
of many books all rolled up into one.*

THE JESUS TWELVE (PLUS JUDAS AND PAUL)

While Jesus had many disciples (students and followers) the Bible focuses particularly on 12 who were closest to him. Tradition says that these 12 spread Jesus' message throughout the known world (Matthew 28:18-20). For this reason, they were known as *apostles*, a word that means "sent ones."

1 Andrew

A fisherman and the first disciple to follow Jesus, Andrew brought his brother, Simon Peter, to Jesus.

2 Bartholomew

Also called Nathanael, tradition has it that he was martyred by being skinned alive.

3 James the Elder

James, with John and Peter, was one of Jesus' closest disciples. Herod Agrippa killed James because of his faith, which made James a martyr (Acts 12:2).

4 John

John (or one of his followers) is thought to be the author of the Gospel of John and three letters of John. He probably died of natural causes in old age.

5 Matthew

Matthew was a tax collector and, therefore, probably an outcast even among his own people. He is attributed with the authorship of the Gospel of Matthew.

6 Peter

Peter was a fisherman who was brought to faith by his brother Andrew. He was probably martyred in Rome by being crucified upside down.

7 Philip

Philip, possibly a Greek, is responsible for bringing Bartholomew (Nathanael) to faith. He is thought to have died in a city called Phrygia.

8 James the Less

James was called "the Less" so he wouldn't be confused with James, the brother of John, or James, Jesus' brother.

9 Simon

Simon is often called "the Zealot." Zealots were a political group in Jesus' day that favored the overthrow of the Roman government by force.

10 Jude

Jude may have worked with Simon the Zealot in Persia (Iran) where they were martyred on the same day.

11 Thomas

"Doubting" Thomas preached the message of Jesus in India.

12 Matthias

Matthias was chosen by lot to replace Judas. It is thought that he worked mostly in Ethiopia.

⓭ Judas Iscariot

Judas was the treasurer for Jesus' disciples and the one who betrayed Jesus for 30 pieces of silver. According to the Bible, Judas killed himself for his betrayal.

⓮ Paul

Paul is considered primarily responsible for bringing non-Jewish people to faith in Jesus. He traveled extensively and wrote many letters to believers. Many of Paul's letters are included in the New Testament.

THE FOUR WEIRDEST LAWS IN THE OLD TESTAMENT

The Old Testament has many helpful, common sense laws, such as "You shall not kill," and, "You shall not steal." Christians sometimes (rightly) accuse one another of picking and choosing which of the Old Testament laws to obey. Alas, United Methodists have been known to emphasize a law that agreed with their preconceptions while ignoring the next law that was inconvenient. Picking among moral laws and cultural laws and ceremonial laws is not easy pickings. Try these on for size:

1 The "ox" law.

"When an ox gores a man or a woman to death, the ox shall be stoned, and its flesh shall not be eaten; but the owner of the ox shall not be liable" (Exodus 21:28). It is about protecting others from reckless actions and thoughtless revenge. Read the next verse (Exodus 21:29). Results get a bit, uh, more permanent for a repeat offender.

2 The "no kid boiling" law.

"You shall not boil a kid in its mother's milk" (Exodus 23:19b). A "kid," of course, is a juvenile goat, not a human being.

3 The "which bugs are legal to eat" law.

"All winged insects that walk upon all fours are detestable to you. But among the winged insects that walk on all fours you may eat those that have jointed legs above their feet" (Leviticus 11:20-21). The law is unclear whether it is legal to eat the bug if you first pull off the legs.

People living in biblical times were sometimes gored by oxen.

❹ The "pure cloth" law.

"You shall not wear clothes made of wool and linen woven together" (Deuteronomy 22:11). Polyester came along after Bible times.

THE TOP TEN BIBLE MIRACLES AND WHAT THEY MEAN

❶ Creation.

God created the universe and everything that is in it, and God continues to create and recreate without ceasing. God's first and ongoing miracle was to reveal that the creation has a purpose.

❷ The Passover.

The Israelites were enslaved by Pharaoh, a ruler who believed the people belonged to him, not to God. In the last of ten plagues, God visited the houses of all the Egyptians to kill the firstborn male in each one. God alone is Lord of the people, and no human can claim ultimate power over us.

❸ The Exodus.

God's people were fleeing Egypt when Pharaoh dispatched his army to force them back into slavery. The army trapped the people with their backs to a sea, but God parted the water and the people walked across to freedom while Pharaoh's minions were destroyed. God chose to free us from all forms of tyranny so we may use that freedom to serve God and each other.

❹ Manna.

After the people crossed the sea to freedom, they complained that they were going to starve to death. They even asked to go back to Egypt. God sent manna, a form of bread, so the people lived. Do you suppose some complained because the manna came without butter and jam? God cares for us even when we give up, pine for our slavery, and lose faith. God never abandons us.

⑤ The Incarnation.
The immortal and infinite God became a human being, choosing to be born of a woman. God loved us enough to become one of us in Jesus of Nazareth, forever bridging the divide that had separated us from God.

⑥ Jesus healed the paralyzed man.
Some men brought a paralyzed friend to Jesus. Jesus said, "Son, your sins are forgiven" (Mark 2:5). This means that Jesus has the power to forgive our sins—and he does so as a free gift.

⑦ Jesus calmed the storm.
Jesus was asleep in a boat with his disciples when a great storm came up and threatened to sink it. He said, "Peace! Be still!" (Mark 4:39). Then the storm immediately calmed. Jesus is Lord over even the powers of nature.

⑧ The Resurrection.
Human beings executed Jesus, but God raised him from the dead on the third day. Through baptism, we share in Jesus' death, so we will also share in eternal life with God the Father, Son, and Holy Spirit. Christ conquered death.

⑨ Pentecost.
Jesus ascended from the earth, but he did not leave the church powerless or alone. On the 50th day after the Jewish Passover (*Pentecost* means 50th), Jesus sent the Holy Spirit to create the church and take up residence among us. The Holy Spirit is present with us always.

⑩ The Final Coming.
One day, Christ will come again and end all suffering. This means that the final result of the epic battle between good and evil is already assured. It is simply that evil has not yet admitted defeat.

NOAH'S ARK

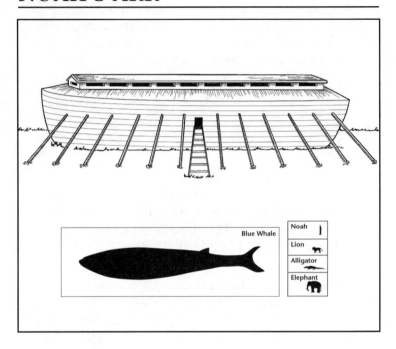

Blue Whale

Noah
Lion
Alligator
Elephant

A cubit is equal to the length of a man's forearm from the elbow to the tip of the middle finger—approximately 18 inches or 45.7 centimeters. Noah's ark was 300 cubits long, 50 cubits wide, and 30 cubits tall (Genesis 6:15).

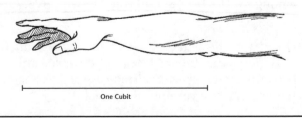

One Cubit

THE EXODUS

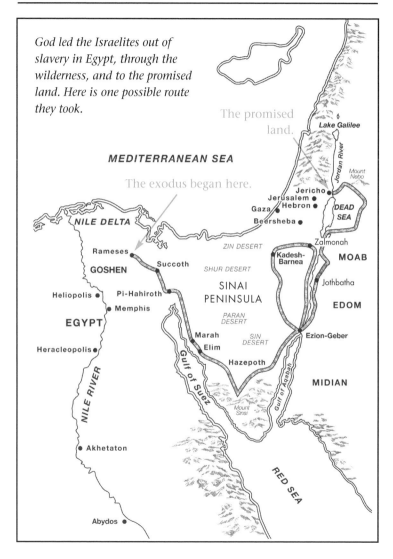

God led the Israelites out of slavery in Egypt, through the wilderness, and to the promised land. Here is one possible route they took.

The promised land.

Lake Galilee

MEDITERRANEAN SEA

The exodus began here.

Jordan River

Mount Nebo

Jerusalem •

Jericho •

NILE DELTA

Gaza / Hebron •

DEAD SEA

Beersheba •

Rameses •

ZIN DESERT

Zalmonah

Succoth

GOSHEN

SHUR DESERT

Kadesh-Barnea •

MOAB

Heliopolis •

Pi-Hahiroth

SINAI PENINSULA

• Memphis

PARAN DESERT

Jothbatha

EDOM

EGYPT

Marah

SIN DESERT

Heracleopolis •

Elim

Ezion-Geber

Hazepoth

Gulf of Suez

Gulf of Aqaba

MIDIAN

Mount Sinai

NILE RIVER

• Akhetaton

RED SEA

• Abydos

THE ARK OF THE COVENANT

God told the Israelites to place the stone tablets—the "covenant"—of the law into the Ark of the Covenant. The Israelites believed that God was invisibly enthroned above the vessel and went before them wherever they traveled.

The Ark of the Covenant was 2.5 cubits long and 1.5 cubits wide (Exodus 25:17).

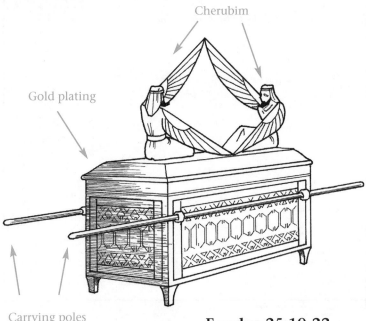

Cherubim

Gold plating

Carrying poles

Exodus 25:10-22

SOLOMON'S TEMPLE

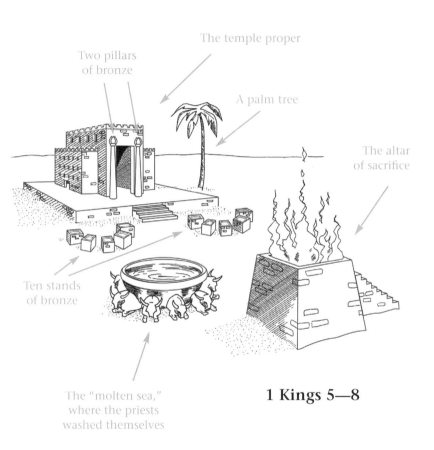

The temple proper

Two pillars
of bronze

A palm tree

The altar
of sacrifice

Ten stands
of bronze

The "molten sea,"
where the priests
washed themselves

1 Kings 5—8

THE HOLY LANDS—
OLD TESTAMENT TIMES

THE HOLY LANDS—
NEW TESTAMENT TIMES

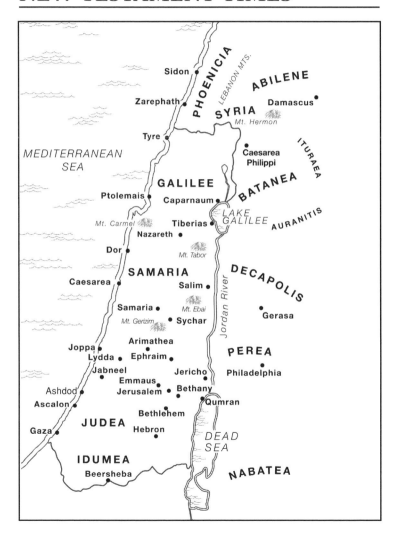

JERUSALEM IN JESUS' TIME

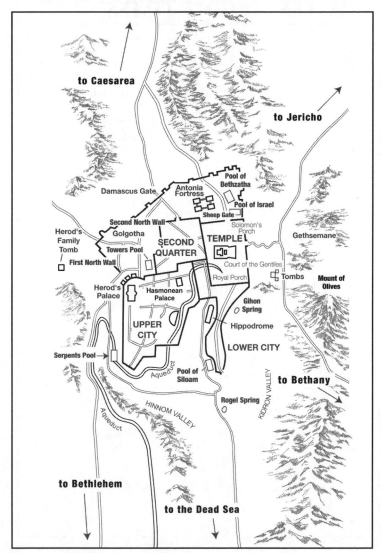

to Caesarea

to Jericho

Pool of Bethzatha

Antonia Fortress

Damascus Gate

Pool of Israel

Second North Wall

Sheep Gate

Solomon's Porch

Golgotha

Herod's Family Tomb

SECOND QUARTER

TEMPLE

Gethsemane

Towers Pool

First North Wall

Court of the Gentiles

Royal Porch

Tombs

Mount of Olives

Herod's Palace

Hasmonean Palace

Gihon Spring

Hippodrome

UPPER CITY

LOWER CITY

Serpents Pool

Aqueduct

Pool of Siloam

to Bethany

HINNOM VALLEY

Rogel Spring

KIDRON VALLEY

Aqueduct

to Bethlehem

to the Dead Sea

THE ARMOR OF GOD

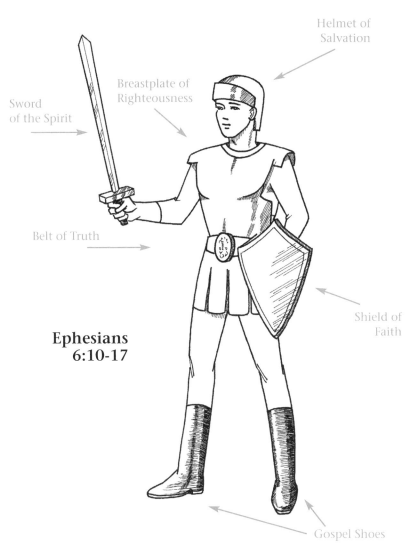

Helmet of
Salvation

Breastplate of
Righteousness

Sword
of the Spirit

Belt of Truth

Shield of
Faith

**Ephesians
6:10-17**

Gospel Shoes

PAUL'S JOURNEYS

Paul traveled extensively, making four separate journeys to spread the gospel to people in other parts of the world. ⟶

- - - - - - - - - - - 1st Journey

———————— 2nd Journey

···························· 3rd Journey

- - - - - - - - - - - - 4th Journey

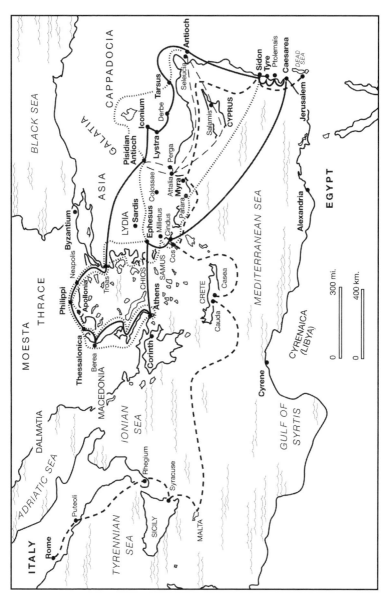

THE PASSION AND CRUCIFIXION

Judas betrayed Jesus with a kiss, saying, "the one I will kiss is the man; arrest him" (Matthew 26:48).

Peter denied Jesus three times (Matthew 26:69-75).

After being flogged, carrying the patibulum was nearly impossible for Jesus.

*Crucifixion was so common in Jesus'
time that the Romans had special
names for the parts of the cross.*

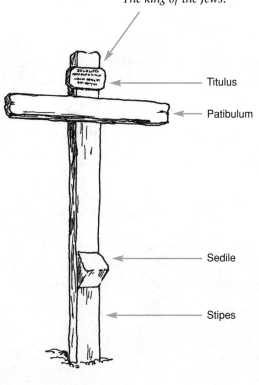

*The charge against Jesus read,
"The king of the Jews."*

Titulus

Patibulum

Sedile

Stipes

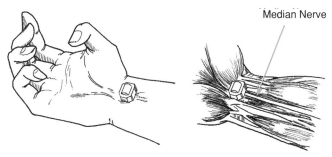

Median Nerve

Typical crucifixion involved being nailed to the cross through the wrists— an excruciatingly painful and humiliating punishment.

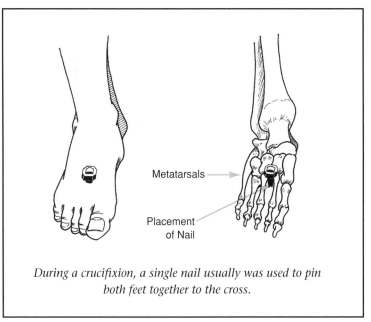

Metatarsals

Placement of Nail

During a crucifixion, a single nail usually was used to pin both feet together to the cross.

Eventually, the victim would be unable to lift himself to take a breath, and he would suffocate. Although our sensibilities and sense of respect do not allow us to depict crucifixions in this manner, the victims were further humiliated by being stripped of all clothing.

While the Romans broke the legs of the men who were crucified next to Jesus, they found that Jesus had already died. To make sure, they pierced his side with a spear, probably to puncture his heart (John 19:34).

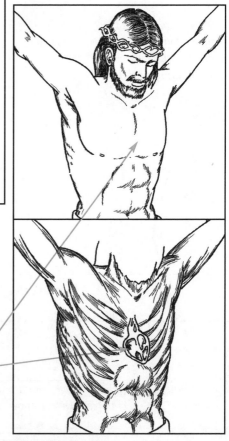

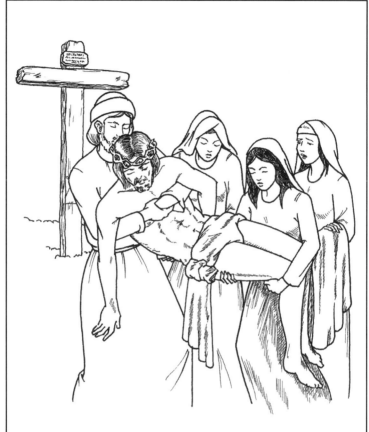

Joseph of Arimathea and several women took Jesus down and carried him to the tomb (Matthew 27:57-61).

The miracle of resurrection took place three days later, when Jesus rose from the dead.

UNITED METHODIST STUFF

The United Methodist story is filled with many twists and turns. When the movement has been at its best, it has been the turns of God that have redirected United Methodism and the predecessor denominations. When the movement has slipped from its best, it has been the twists of human pride and error that have stalled or simply failed.

United Methodists have a reputation for massive record keeping. (How many left-handed people from Switzerland attended church in Nebraska during the month of August? What is the average attendance at meetings held on the second floor of buildings less than ten years old? How often did the pastor use the words "connectional system" during the week preceding charge conference?) Your own questions might have emerged.

- What's the deal with all those statistics?
- What is a charge conference? (And, how much is the charge? Do you take credit cards?)

- Is there anything that some United Methodist somewhere doesn't believe?

- How does God get in touch with United Methodists?

- Why isn't a local pastor the same thing as the pastor of a local church?

- What mission is causing United Methodists to do what they do?

- Why do some Methodists say they aren't United Methodists?

- Which works better for pressing dried flowers: the Bible or *The Book of Discipline of The United Methodist Church?*

  That's probably enough questions to get us through to the end of the book. If not, you can always add the question asked by Charles Wesley in a hymn: "How can we sinners know our sins on earth forgiven?"

THE MEANS OF GRACE

Whether it was Martin Boehm's faithful preaching of the Word or Jacob Albright's small groups studying the Scripture or John Wesley's gathering early Methodists together in conference or Philip William Otterbein's inviting to the Lord's Table those who were seeking salvation, United Methodist people have rejoiced in finding those ways that God gives grace to God's people.

John Wesley once referred to these acts as "ordinary means of grace." By that, he meant that this is the way that God ordinarily gives grace, but there are no limits to be put upon God. If God chooses to grant grace in some other way, some extraordinary way, it is indeed God's to give. Nevertheless, scriptural promise and the experience of believers have led the church to name certain ways that God gives grace—the means of grace.

❶ Holy Communion.

United Methodists put this sacrament in the center of the life of the community of faith. And why not? This is more than just recalling what Jesus did "back then"; in this bread and cup is the Real Presence of our Lord. That is what Jesus declared when he said, "This is my body. This is my blood." Jesus' presence is spiritual. (The bread remains bread; the juice remains juice.) But the presence is real and United Methodists are called to come constantly to the Lord's Table. It is a means of grace.

❷ Public Worship of God.

United Methodist churches sometimes have no youth; some have no children; some have no Sunday School; some have no service projects; some have no building; some have no ordained pastor. But one thing all United

Methodist congregations do: they have public worship. In fact, *The Book of Discipline* spells out that a pastor cannot simply stop having services of worship. The definition of a local church includes: "the church exists for the maintenance of worship." It is a means of grace.

❸ Ministry of the Word.
The Protestant tradition has long emphasized that access to the Scriptures is a gift that should be available to all. Studying the Bible, hearing sermons which explore the Scriptures, spending time in reading the Bible—these are all ways United Methodists encounter the living God in the living Word. God chooses to bless these engagements with Scripture. As the confession of faith Otterbein prepared for his Baltimore congregation read, "every true Christian is bound to acknowledge and receive (the Bible) with the influence of the Spirit of God." It is a means of grace.

❹ Family and Private Prayer.
Any reading of the early journals of the ancestors of United Methodism will reveal that these stalwarts took part in personal and family devotional time. Even when traveling, Francis Asbury (one of the first Methodist bishops) would join with host families for prayer. Jacob Albright reported spending hours in prayer with friends and family. Martin Boehm would fall to his knees in the field to offer intense prayer. Barbara Heck insisted that early Methodists in New York give seasons to prayer and preaching. These were conversations with God. It is a means of grace.

❺ Fasting.
Truth to tell, other than giving up an occasional slice of cheesecake or resorting to drinking only diet soft drinks,

most United Methodists have lost the tradition of fasting. Jacob Albright wrote that he always found fasting and prayer "to be the best means in the hour of trial." United Methodist clergy in full connection have all promised to recommend fasting by precept and example. John Wesley fasted twice a week (from sunrise to midafternoon on Wednesdays and Fridays). Wesley said fasting helps in prayer and with identifying with the hungry; besides, God commands fasting and promises to reward it. It is a means of grace.

⑥ Conferencing.

Because United Methodists believe that God most often grants faith and gives grace through the community of faith and grace, The United Methodist Church seeks to be such a community, a connection. The denominational structure is a series of conferences. (More on that in "Organized to Beat the Devil" on page 223.) The defining terms from Methodist and United Brethren and Evangelical history are relational terms: class, bands, societies, meetings, association, connection (or connexion), and conference. If not in person, the dialogue was to be through books (John Dickins—Methodist, and John Dreisbach—Evangelical, being key to American publishing). As early as 1744, John Wesley called together Methodist leaders for accountability and conversation and conferencing about what to teach, how to teach, and what to do. Why not conferencing? It is a means of grace.

⑦ Works of Mercy.

God is pleased to convey grace even beyond the ordinary ordinances of God—works of piety (as discussed above). There are works of mercy which are also means of grace.

Clothing the naked! Feeding the hungry! Refreshing the thirsty! Visiting the prisoner! Welcoming the stranger! (Matthew 25:31-46). John Wesley went so far as to write, "[Good works] are the highest part of that spiritual building whereof Jesus Christ in the foundation." Nevertheless, apart from the power of God, there is no power in good deeds. These works are not a way to win God's favor, but when we, in the words of John Wesley, "do all the good (we) can," God can pour out abundant gifts. It is a means of grace.

ONE BAD JOKE AND SOME SERIOUS MATTERS

Disclaimer: The author of this account is well aware that this description is based on unfair stereotypes and that you have three cousins who know more about this than the author. Maybe this falls into the category of things that did not happen but are still true. Maybe.

A group of laypeople were enjoying an ecumenical breakfast and discussing how things had gone the day before at their respective churches.

- The Baptist said, "My preacher began his sermon with great energy by saying, 'The Bible says!'"

- The Roman Catholic said, "My priest began by saying 'Church tradition has taught us . . .'"

- The Pentecostal said, "Our preacher started the sermon, 'The Holy Spirit has revealed to me . . .'"

- The Episcopalian said, "My rector said, "According to the *Book of Common Prayer* . . .'"

- The United Methodist said, "Our pastor started off, 'It seems to me . . .'"

(Pause for polite chuckle.)

Some friends of the family have said that United Methodists concentrate so much on *doing* that they do not have much time for *thinking*. Do United Methodists have anything more to say than "It seems to me"? Do United Methodists have standards for doctrine?

Yes! When The United Methodist Church was formed in 1968, the Plan of Union accepted four documents to represent the doctrinal standards: (1) John Wesley's *Explanatory Notes Upon the New Testament*, (2) John Wesley's *Standard Sermons*, (3) the Confession of Faith of the Evangelical United Brethren Church, and (4) the Articles of Religion of The Methodist Church. Each of these items is understood to be rooted in and expressive of Scripture.

From the earliest days of the Methodist movement and its companion communities of faith, the United Brethren Church and the Evangelical Association, there was a common theology. Preachers were expected to pass on those teachings and none other. The congregation in Baltimore pastored by Philip William Otterbein had this in its Constitution: "No preacher shall stay among us who teacheth the doctrine of predestination or the impossibility of falling from grace, and who holdeth them as doctrinal points." In the twenty-first century, clergy and laypeople alike can be (but seldom are) brought to church trial for "dissemination of doctrines contrary to the established standards of doctrine of The United Methodist Church." Pastors are tested on their theology before being given license to preach. This is a far cry from "It seems to me"!

Explanatory Notes Upon the New Testament

In this extensive volume (over a thousand pages), John Wesley prepared commentary and interpretation of the New Testament "chiefly for the plain, unlettered [persons], who understand only their mother-tongue, and yet reverence and love the Word of God, and have a desire to save their souls."

Standard Sermons

As a teaching tool, John Wesley released collections of his sermons. The topics ranged from the meaning of new birth to perfection to Christian charity to conversion to social witness to Holy Communion to baptism to repentance to sin to a generous spirit to the Sermon on the Mount . . . and more.

Confession of Faith

The 1962 General Conference of the Evangelical United Brethren Church approved this statement of faith. It updated language, but did not change the doctrinal trust of the predecessor United Brethren Church and Evangelical Church. Because these denominations had paralleled Methodist teaching, it was not difficult for The United Methodist Church (in 1968) to accept the Confession of Faith as a doctrinal standard.

Articles of Religion

In 1784, John Wesley sent the American Methodists his revision of the Articles of Religion (doctrines) of the Church of England. In 1808, the *Discipline* of the American church adopted the 25 articles as one of its doctrinal standards. Ever since then, a restrictive rule in the Constitution has effectively blocked any change in these articles.

How much sleep do you want tonight?

The assumption here is that you want to go to bed sometime before it is time to get up. In solidarity with that view, *The Unofficial United Methodist Handbook* will not duplicate the text of all four of these standards. (This decision saves you about 2,138 pages and saves the American forests a bunch of trees.) Check out a library or rummage around the Internet or call your pastor (4:00 a.m. ought to do it). It's good stuff; there is just a lot of it.

TWENTY-FIVE THINGS THAT REALLY MATTER

As a sampler of these official United Methodist doctrinal standards, here are the titles of the 25 articles that form the Articles of Religion. Rather than printing the full text of the articles, each title is followed by a brief summary. The language of the articles reflects images and gender terms of earlier centuries. The social and ecumenical context today invites United Methodists to relate these teachings in a world that is different from the one in which they were written. Notes in *italics* offer a perspective on the history out of which the article emerged.

• **Article I—Of Faith in the Holy Trinity**

God does not have physical parts. The Father, Son, and Holy Spirit are co-equal and co-eternal.

• **Article II—Of the Word, or Son of God, Who Was Made Very Man**

The Son joins perfect human and perfect divine natures in one person. His death reconciled the Father to us and was a sacrifice for our sins.

• **Article III—Of the Resurrection of Christ**

Christ rose from the dead, ascended into heaven, and will return to judge all people at the last day.

• **Article IV—Of the Holy Ghost**

The Holy Spirit proceeds from the Father and the Son and is co-equal and co-eternal with them.

- **Article V—Of the Sufficiency of the Holy Scriptures for Salvation**

  The Holy Scripture contains all we need to know for salvation. Thirty-nine Old Testament books and 27 New Testament books make up the canon.

- **Article VI—Of the Old Testament**

  The Old Testament speaks of the same God as the New Testament. Christians are not bound by the Old Testament's ceremonial and civil law, but by the moral law of the Old Testament.

- **Article VII—Of Original or Birth Sin**

  God created humankind in original righteousness, but the offspring of Adam have a corrupted nature always inclined to evil.

- **Article VIII—Of Free Will**

  God in Christ gives us grace by which we may seek and call upon God. The gift of a free will is a mark of God's prevenient (going before) grace. *This statement was in contrast to those who argued that God picked those to be saved.*

- **Article IX—Of the Justification of Man**

  The only righteousness we have before God is the merit of Jesus Christ. We are justified (made right) with God only through faith.

- **Article X—Of Good Works**

  Good works cannot save us. A true and lively faith is evidenced in good works. They are, as it were, the fruits of faith.

- **Article XI—Of Works of Supererogation**

  Trying to add on to the commandments of God is arrogant and lacks true piety. Works beyond what God commands are empty.

• **Article XII—Of Sin After Justification**

Even after we have been justified and pardoned of our sin, we can still fall into sin. Repentance is still possible after we fall from saving grace. *In contrast to this teaching, there were persons who claimed "once saved, always saved."*

• **Article XIII—Of the Church**

The visible church is a congregation where there is faith, where the pure Word of God is preached, and the Sacraments are duly administered.

• **Article XIV—Of Purgatory**

The Scripture does not speak of purgatory or asking favors of saints or maintaining relics. These are human inventions. *In eighteenth-century England, there was great enmity between Roman Catholics and Protestants. This article expresses some of that division.*

• **Article XV—Of Speaking in the Congregation in Such a Tongue as the People Understand**

The primitive church did not allow public prayers or the administration of the Sacraments in a language the people did not understand. *This was a statement against the Roman Catholic use of Latin in their services.*

• **Article XVI—Of the Sacraments**

The Lord's Supper and Baptism are the only Sacraments instituted by our Lord with physical sign and a promise of grace. Sacraments bring strength to faith. *This article spoke against those traditions that recognized confirmation, penance, ordination, matrimony, and extreme unction as sacraments.*

- **Article XVII—Of Baptism**

  Baptism is a sign of new birth, marking a difference between Christians and those not baptized. The practice of baptizing infants is to be retained. *This article was aimed at those who baptized only adult believers.*

- **Article XVIII—Of the Lord's Supper**

  Through faith, receiving the bread and the cup is partaking of the redemptive body and blood of Jesus. The Supper is a sign of the love Christians have for each other.

- **Article XIX—Of Both Kinds**

  Both the cup and the bread should be made available to laypeople, administered to all Christians alike. *A common Roman Catholic practice at this time was to allow only the clergy to drink the wine.*

- **Article XX—Of the One Oblation of Christ, Finished Upon the Cross**

  The one offering (oblation) of Christ upon the cross is a sufficient sacrifice for the sins of the world. *This article spoke against those who offered each mass (Communion service) as a new sacrifice of Christ.*

- **Article XXI—Of the Marriage of Ministers**

  Clergy are as free to marry as any other Christian who thinks marriage is the best way to serve God. *Roman Catholics denied marriage to their priests; early Methodist leaders sometimes discouraged marriage by the preachers for fear that marriage would divert their attention from gospel work.*

- **Article XXII—Of the Rites and Ceremonies of Churches**

  Rites and ceremonies do not have to be alike everywhere,

but unless provoked by the Word of God, no one should break the practices of his or her church.

- **Article XXIII—Of the Rulers of the United States of America**

  The Constitution of the United States along with the delegated leaders of the states and of the United States shall not be subject to foreign jurisdiction. *It was important that Methodists in America (1784) be seen as loyal to the new country and now separated from any authority in England.*

- **Article XXIV—Of Christian Men's Goods**

  The property of Christians is not commonly held property, but every one should give liberally to help the poor.

- **Article XXV—Of a Christian Man's Oath**

  Christian religion, while prohibiting vain and rash swearing, does allow a Christian to swear an oath when the courts require it for justice, judgment, and truth.

FOUR WAYS TO THINK THEOLOGICALLY— NO, MAKE THAT FIVE

If you want to be impressive in United Methodist circles, occasionally drop the term "Wesleyan quadrilateral" into your conversation. Those who understand what that means will admire you for your theological competence; those who do not know what it means will respect you for your arcane wisdom. You can't lose.

For starters, neither John nor Charles Wesley used the term "quadrilateral." (As a matter of fact, neither did Samuel Wesley, Susannah Wesley, Mehetabel Wesley, Kezia Wesley, Mary Wesley, Emilia Wesley, nor Wesley Hardin nor Wesley Wesley.) Probably, it was Dr. Albert Outler, a twentieth-century scholar, who came up with the term to describe four ingredients—four sides, quadrilateral—in the best thinking of those in the Wesleyan tradition.

These four considerations are the guidelines (sources, criteria) for United Methodist theological reflection. The goal, as stated in *The Book of Discipline* is to "reflect critically on our biblical and theological inheritance, striving to express faithfully the witness we make in our own time."

❶ Scripture

Scripture is primary. Individual texts are read in light of how they fit into the whole message of the Bible. The Bible contains all that is necessary for salvation. The Holy Spirit guides the use of scholarly insight in order to apply the original context and intention of a passage to today's circumstance. *The Book of Discipline* states that the Bible is not only a source for our faith but also is "the basic criterion by which the truth and fidelity of any interpretation of faith is measured."

❷ Tradition

We are not the first generation to engage in theological thought, so there is much to be learned from those who have thought before us. John Wesley gave great value not only to the New Testament witness but also to those who clarified doctrine and teaching in the first two or three centuries of the church. (He also accepted the traditional faith statements of the eighteenth-century Church of England.) To ignore the common history of the church would be arrogant and unproductive.

❸ Experience

Experience confirms what the Scriptures say about the grace of God. The varied nature of the Christian experience makes it difficult to draw the boundaries for how God works. Early publications in the Methodist, Evangelical, and United Brethren journeys often told personal stories of faith: experience of heroes and heroines of faith. Experience is not only personal but also corporate. In fact, *The Book of Discipline* recognizes that "God's gift of liberating love embraces the whole of creation."

❹ Reason

God is beyond the capacity of human thought, but the discipline of theology calls for the use of reason. Reason enables believers to organize faithful witness. Reason helps test how our witness and tradition matches Scripture. Reason gives tools for reading Scripture. All truth comes from God, so United Methodists usually have no fear in exploring new avenues of thought. Such reasoning asks questions that open doors to God's further revelation.

Scripture. Tradition. Experience. Reason. Those four components comprise the best United Methodist theological expression. *The Book of Discipline* declares that John Wesley "believed that the living core of the Christian faith was revealed in Scripture, illumined by tradition, vivified in personal experience, and confirmed by reason."

That's four ways to think theologically. What about the fifth?

⑤ Number Five

These four sources of theology need a fifth dimension: talking with each other. Scripture is always the principal player in the conversation as well as being the *principle* player, but it is in dialogue/trialogue with the others. No one of these guidelines stands alone. What can experience learn from tradition? How can Scripture move us beyond reason? What do reason and tradition have to say to each other? It is in the interrelatedness of these four aspects that United Methodist theology makes its clearest contribution. Scripture is always the determining factor, but Scripture, Tradition, Experience, and Reason are on the journey together.

The Interdependence of the Four Elements of Wesley's Quadrilateral

We rely on the way of salvation given in the Bible.

We use the Bible as a touchstone in examining real or supposed revelation.

We take it as the final authority in matters of faith and practice.

Thus we need to study and interpret it carefully.

Roots: Protestant Reformation

Danger: bibliolatry

We revere the ancient church as well as our own.

We use the writings of Christians through the centuries.

Particular value is given to the early church fathers.

The standards of the Church of England are utilized; prayerbook and homilies.

Roots: Roman Catholic Church

Danger: traditionalism

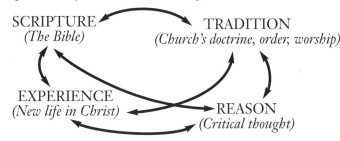

SCRIPTURE
(The Bible)

TRADITION
(Church's doctrine, order, worship)

EXPERIENCE
(New life in Christ)

REASON
(Critical thought)

The Holy Spirit uses scripture and tradition to bring us to faith.

By God's grace we receive a personal experience of faith.

There are variations of Christian experience; none can be normative.

Thus ours is a "heart religion," but it is not dependent on "feelings."

Roots: free churches

Danger: "enthusiasm"

Reason lays the foundation for true religion and helps raise its superstructure.

Reason helps us order the evidence of revelation and (with tradition) guard against poor interpretation of scripture.

But reason cannot prove or disclose God.

Roots: deism

Danger: rationalism

—From Lovett H. Weems Jr., *John Wesley's Message Today* (Nashville: Abingdon Press, 1991), 13.

TEAR OUT THIS PAGE AND HIDE IT ON YOUR PERSON

You can never tell when a stranger will come up to you on the street and ask, "What are some distinctive theological emphases among United Methodists?" After you mumble something about "always taking up an offering" and "they eat a lot," you begin to wish for a quick reference guide. This page is your answer sheet. Tear it out and keep it nearby. When that stranger walks up, you'll be ready.

- **Assurance:** Ordinarily, when a person is justified (receives God's pardon for sins), God gives that person an assurance of forgiveness.

- **Catholic Spirit:** Here the word "catholic" means universal. United Methodist heritage allows for a variety of opinions and does not insist on total agreement while holding to basic essentials. It is a generous spirit.

- **Christian Perfection:** John Wesley said that Jesus meant it when our Lord said, "Be perfect as your father in heaven is perfect." Such perfection does not mean without mistake. It means complete love of God and complete love of neighbor.

- **Fall from Grace:** People may lose their faith in Christ (and thus lose their justification).

- **Free Will:** God has given grace to every person by which that person may freely accept (or reject) God's offer of salvation.

- **Holiness:** The fullness of salvation is expressed in holy living (sanctification).

- **Justifying Grace:** God graciously moves to bring people back into a right relationship with God (justified). Sin is pardoned. This grace is appropriated through faith.

- **Means of Grace:** These are the ways that God ordinarily chooses to give grace: Lord's Supper, prayer, Scripture, fasting, worship, conferencing, and acts of mercy.

- **Mission:** Salvation involves more than a personal relationship with God. It connects to love of neighbor, passion for justice, and global concern.

- **Prevenient Grace:** Coming from the Latin word for "coming before," prevenient grace is God's work in every human being, coming before we know it, recognize it, or claim it.

- **Sanctifying Grace:** God gives grace (undeserved gift) by which believers are able to grow in grace, moving on to perfection or entire sanctification.

- **Works:** The evidence of faith is good works. Works do not earn salvation but are the fruits of salvation.

Department of Disclaimer

United Methodists are not the only Christians who believe and practice most of these affirmations. They are listed here because these matters get priority in the United Methodist expedition.

There are, of course, other beliefs which United Methodists embrace as part of the larger Christian family: salvation through Jesus Christ, activity of the Holy Spirit, church as the body of Christ, God's present and future reign, and authority of Scripture. Want to know more? Read "Doctrinal Standards and Our Theological Task" in *The Book of Discipline.*

UNITED METHO-SPEAK

Can you talk in United Metho-speak? Like most communities, United Methodists have their own "in house" jargon. Such insider vocabulary can be confusing both to member and non-member. How about testing your readiness to translate from Metho-speak?

Here is an (incomplete!) series of abbreviations, acronyms, and titles used within The United Methodist Church. If you know the meaning, fill in the blank. If not, check your local phone directory and call an unsuspecting United Methodist church and ask for a translator. Or, you can simply read the answers at the end of the list.

(1) AC _____

(2) CAH _____

(3) CEF _____

(4) COB _____

(5) CORR _____

(6) COSROW _____

(7) DCA _____

(8) EMLC _____

(9) GBCS _____

(10) GBGM _____

(11) GBOD _____

(12) GBOPHB _____

(13) GCFA _____

(14) MARCHA _____

(15) MEF _____

(16) NAIC _____

(17) SEJ _____

(18) UMCOR _____

(19) UMM _____

(20) UMPH _____

(21) UMW _____

(22) UMYF _____

(23) YSF _____

(24) PPRC _____

(25) ZYT _____

Check out your answers:

(1) Annual Conference; (2) Commission on Archives and History; (3) Christian Educators Fellowship; (4) Council of Bishops; (5) Commission on Religion and Race; (6) Commission on Status and Role of Women; (7) *Daily Christian Advocate*—printed at General Conference; (8) Ethnic Minority Local Church; (9) General Board of Church and Society; (10) General Board of Global Ministries; (11) General Board of Discipleship; (12) General Board of Pension and Health Benefits; (13) General Council on Finance and Administration; (14) Methodistas Associados Representado la Causa de los Hispano Americanos—Methodists Associated Representing the Cause of Hispanic Americans; (15) Ministerial Education Fund; (16) Native American International Caucus; (17) Southeastern Jurisdiction; (18) United Methodist Committee on Relief; (19) United Methodist Men; (20) United Methodist Publishing House; (21) United Methodist Women; (22) United Methodist Youth Fellowship; (23) Youth Service Fund; (24) Pastor-Parish Relations Committee (25) This one does not exist; it is provided to see what creative answer you might have supplied.

ORGANIZED TO BEAT THE DEVIL

In the early days of the forerunners of United Methodism, the movement was said to be "organized to beat the devil." Organized, for sure. The book of church law for The United Methodist Church *(The Book of Discipline of The United Methodist Church 2004)* is nearly 850 pages long. The index alone runs eighty-five pages, ranging from "abandonment of local church property" to "Youth Service Fund—promotion by General Commission on Communication."

❶ Why have all these detailed instructions about being United Methodist?

From the days of Boehm, Albright, Otterbein, and Wesley(s), this tradition has operated within the framework of Christian accountability. When the family was smaller, this answerability took place in small, face-to-face encounters. As the ministry expanded, these direct engagements became more difficult, so together the members set standards and rules by which they would agree to live their lives, even when apart from one another. To quote *The Discipline* as it paraphrases John Wesley: "Solitary religion is invalid."

❷ How do people I don't know have an idea of what is best for me?

In a denomination that gives major priority to faith as a community journey, it is not surprising that the focus is on what is "best for us" rather than what is "best for me." The question becomes "How does our entire United Methodist family serve Christ?" Each member of the family has a different view depending on where he or she is standing. To get the best overall view, all of these perceptions have to be brought together and rubbed together until there is a common vision. All of us know more than any one of us.

❸ How do individuals and local churches fit into this big picture?

The big picture is individuals and local churches. When The United Methodist Church makes decisions that impact the total family, those decisions are made by the same individuals from the same local churches that make up the connection. (See the chart about annual conference and general conference.) *The Book of Discipline* is filled with ways individuals and local churches access the decision-making settings. For example, any member or local congregation can petition the General Conference to change *The Book of Discipline.* There is an appeal process when clergy or laypersons do not agree with charges brought against them. There is an appeal process when a local church does not want to accept a decision made by a denominational district board on church location and building. There is a consultation with pastors and a local church committee before pastoral assignments are made. Congregations are given wide flexibility in how best to organize locally to be in mission. But, as effective football players and successful basketball players know, it is ultimately not "what I want" but what works best for the team.

❹ How is The United Methodist Church organized?

To someone unfamiliar with the polity (the way of organizing) of United Methodism, the various churches, conferences, committees might seem like so much clutter.

```
                    Thither

                                Everywhere

Hither    Neither Here

          Here                              Who



                    Where              There

                              Yon

Nor There
```

To those who wander frequently in United Methodist circles, the connectional way of life reflects both the theological understanding of "church" (many members, one body) and the practical shape of mission and ministry (how do things best get done). *The Book of Discipline* describes this connectional voyage as "multi-leveled, global in scope, and local in thrust."

If none of this makes sense, refer to the chart above.

GENERAL CONFERENCE
DISCIPLINE
writes *Book of Discipline*
proposes Constitution
speaks for denomination
links to connection

JURISDICTIONAL CONFERENCE
(OUTSIDE U.S., CENTRAL CONFERENCE)
ELECTS BISHOPS
election of bishops
promotional role
boundaries of annual
    conferences
regional ministry
links to connection

ANNUAL CONFERENCE
BASIC BODY
clergy licensed or ordained
sets regional budget
bishop makes appointments of pastors and deacons
elects delegates to jurisdictional and general conferences
votes on Constitution
undergirds regional ministry
links to connection

DISTRICT CONFERENCE
OPTIONAL
committee to approve
local church building
projects
issues certificate for
candidates for
ordained ministry
district property
links to connection

CHARGE CONFERENCE
MISSION
sets local mission and
ministry
elects local officers
elects lay member(s)
of annual conference
local building projects
approves candidates
for ministry
links to connection

Be Aware

- Committees exist at each level for administration, ministry, outreach, finances, property, planning.

- Institutional ministries (related in a variety of ways to The United Methodist Church) include hospitals, retirement communities, camps, retreat centers, schools, disaster recovery centers, homes for children, investment foundations, communications centers, urban ministry centers, and 4,763 others too numerous to mention.

- Central conferences (outside the United States) have some flexibility to adjust *The Book of Discipline* to fit their special missional settings.

- Each level may assign personnel to work in specialized areas: for example, worship, evangelism, social concerns, stewardship, youth, ethnic life, women's role, pensions, education, ecumenical matters, missions, campus ministry, continuing education, immigration issues, spiritual formation, and if needed, study committees on the value of kumquat production.

STILL ORGANIZING TO BEAT THE DEVIL

If you have lost sleep worrying about conferences, jurisdictions, and kumquat production, be at peace. While this book offers little assistance for the growth of fruit (in spite of the biblical reminder that "by their fruits you shall know them"), it does provide these handy diagrams and charts to help you sort through these matters of United Methodist structure.

The General Conference brings together delegates from all over the world, so only a globe would represent this fact.

In the United States, the jurisdictional conferences divide the country into five regions: western, north central, northeastern, south central, and southeastern. (Quite cleverly, don't you think, the jurisdictions bear the same name as their regions!)

Outside the United States, there are seven central conferences (which function similarly to jurisdictional conferences): Africa Central, Central and Southern Europe, Congo, Germany, Northern Europe, Philippines, and West Africa.

Annual conferences are regional units within the jurisdictional or central conference territories. As an example, here is a map showing the fifteen annual conferences in the South Central Jurisdiction.

South Central Jurisdiction

Be Aware

- Bishops are assigned to episcopal areas that consist of one or more annual conferences.

- A charge conference is usually made up of the elected local church officials, pastor(s), and retired clergy or diaconal ministers related to that charge. (See page 227.)

- With the authorization of the district superintendent, the charge conference can convene as a church conference, with all professing members of the congregation having a vote.

- The traditional opening hymn of annual conference sessions is "And Are We Yet Alive" by Charles Wesley.

- Kumquats can survive at temperatures as low as 14 degrees Fahrenheit.

- A charge may consist of one congregation or of two or more congregations served by the same pastor(s).

- All of the structures of United Methodism exist to achieve the mission of the church: "to make disciples of Jesus Christ."

IS THIS MORE THAN YOU WANT TO KNOW?

If you are finding this excursus into the innards of United Methodism a bit more than you bargained for, you could take time out and go to the annual Kumquat Festival in Dade City, Florida. Otherwise, press on.

The Book of Discipline, the denomination's book of law, is revised every four years by the General Conference. *The Discipline* serves as a book of the covenant among United Methodists to be biblical in faith, inclusive in attitude, and connected in ministry.

What is in The Book of Discipline?

There are nine sections in the 2004 edition. They follow greetings from the bishops, a list of all who have ever been elected bishops in United Methodism (and predecessor groups), and a statement of history.

- The Constitution
- Doctrine, Doctrinal Statements, General Rules, The Ministry of All Christians, and Social Principles
- The Local Church
- The Ministry of the Ordained
- The Superintendency
- The Conferences
- Administrative Order
- Church Property
- Judicial Administration

Be Aware

- Most United Methodists refer to a unit of *The Discipline* by paragraph number rather than page number. This can lead to great sporting events: Who knows the content of paragraph 632.4b(26)? Who can be the first to find paragraph 1421.5c(3)? (It's easier to find the book of Nahum in the Bible.)

- Unless you have a collection of dust, outdated editions of *The Book of Discipline* are of minimal value. Historians. Scholars. UMC geeks. Unless you fit one of those categories, use old *Disciplines* to prop open the side door in the summer time.

- Every four years, the General Conference gives the denomination's official statement on a variety of social issues: poverty, sexuality, war, genetic technology, etc.

- If all of this organization seems highly methodical, keep in mind that the nickname that stuck for the first folks in the movement was "Method-ists." It is in the denominational DNA "to organize to beat the devil."

WE ARE NOT THE ONLY PIG IN THE POKE

(If this image does not register with you, try this: We are not the only game in town. Or, we are not the only name on the dance card.)

United Methodists have great appreciation for and cooperation with the range of the Christian family. After all, each of the early leaders came from another branch of the Christian community and brought gifts from those traditions: Jacob Albright was Lutheran; Martin Boehm was Mennonite; Philip William Otterbein was German Reformed; John and Charles Wesley were Anglicans (Church of England). Otterbein wrote, "The differences of people and denominations end in Christ."

The United Methodist Church is part of all the major inter-denominational groups: National Council of Churches, World Council of Churches, and Churches Uniting in Christ, for example. The United Methodist Church has Interim Eucharistic Sharing agreements with The Episcopal Church and The Evangelical Lutheran Church.

There are Methodists who are not United Methodists. These persons are on other branches of the tree that grew from the ministry of John and Charles Wesley. Here are some illustrations of some of the nearly 100 Methodist denominations gathering over 33 million members in 108 countries. They serve an estimated 70 million persons. They work together in the World Methodist Council.

- African Methodist Episcopal Church—grew out of a late eighteenth-century protest in Philadelphia of racism in American Methodism.

- African Methodist Episcopal Zion Church—emerged in New York City to separate from racism in John Street Methodist Episcopal Church.

- Christian Methodist Episcopal Church—formed in 1870 by former slaves who sought their own church separate from former masters.

- The Free Methodist Church—became separate to maintain an antislavery position and to insist on the doctrine of sanctification.

- Iglesia Methodista del Peru—autonomous for more than 30 years, has an emphasis on education at all levels.

- The Korean Methodist Church—begun in 1884, now including the largest single Methodist congregation in the world (80,000 members).

- The Methodist Church of Great Britain—organized after the death of John Wesley, this denomination is in England, Scotland, and Wales.

- The Wesleyan Church—rooted in revivalism and a strong opposition to slavery, now in more than 50 countries.

  Other denominations, while not part of the World Methodist Council, have a distinctively Methodist flavor in thought and practice. Often there have been historic overlaps with United Methodism.

  - Church of the Nazarene
  - Evangelical Methodist Church
  - Methodist Church of Togo
  - Primitive Methodist Church

LEFTOVER QUESTIONS

Have you ever taken an exam only to discover that the teacher did not ask a single question about the one part of the material you had memorized? (Teacher's Question: "What factors led to the War of 1812?" Your Answer: "Prior to the War of 1812, few people could name the kings of Israel. Those kings were Jehu, Joahaz, Joash, Jereboam II, Zechariah, Shallum, Menahem, Pekahia, and Pekah.")

These questions (and answers) did not seem to fit anywhere else in this book.

- **Q.:** Why do United Methodist preachers move so often?

  A : United Methodist pastors are appointed one year at a time. In a connectional system, pastors are assigned in the way that best serves the entire connection. John Wesley argued that itinerancy (or commonly spelled by some Methodists as itineracy), meaning moving the preachers around, gave each setting access to a needed variety of ministerial gifts.

- **Q.:** "The pastor of my church is not a local pastor." Does that make sense?

  A.: Yes.

- **Q.:** Uh, could you say a bit more?

  A.: "Local pastor" is the term used for those unordained persons who are licensed to serve; they have sacramental authority only in the one place they serve. A pastor who is ordained would not, therefore, be "a local pastor."

- **Q.:** What is the difference between a deacon and an elder?

  A.: An elder is a clergyperson ordained for Word, Order, Sacrament, and Service. A deacon is a clergyperson ordained for Word and Service.

- **Q.:** What is a bishop?

  A.: A bishop is an elder elected (for lifetime) to provide general oversight and supervision. Although a bishop of the whole church, he or she is also assigned a specific area. (A district superintendent is an extension of the bishop's office; for a term, they serve a portion of the bishop's area.)

- **Q.:** How are pastors appointed?

  A.: Each year at annual conference, the bishop assigns the clergy to their stations for the coming year. Some are pastors or deacons in local congregations; some are clergy in extension ministries (teaching, counseling, institutional ministry). After consultation with relevant parties, the bishop (and Cabinet—the district superintendents) determines the best way to deploy the church's personnel. The final decision is that of the bishop.

- **Q.:** Who owns United Methodist property?

  A.: Title to property is held by the local church, annual conference, or institution that owns it. All such property is held in trust for The United Methodist Church; if the property is no longer used for United Methodist purposes, it reverts to the denomination.

- **Q.:** What are the General Rules?

  A.: Early leaders of the ancestors of United Methodism thought those who continued in their religious societies ought to give evidence of their desire of salvation ("the desire to flee the wrath to come") by living holy lives. In the case of Methodists, guidelines for such a life were spelled out in General Rules (still part of United Methodist official documents). In outline, the General Rules say: (a) Do no harm; (b) Do good; (c) Attend upon the ordinances of God.

- **Q.:** Who is the chief bishop, the head of The United Methodist Church?

  A.: There is no "head of The United Methodist Church" (other than Jesus Christ). The bishops choose officers for their work as a Council of Bishops, but their denominational guidance is conciliar (working as a whole Council).

- **Q.:** What are apportionments?

  A.: United Methodists work together and pay together to accomplish common mission. Apportionments are the financial lifeline of these ministries and represent the amount assigned to each entity of the church. A local congregation, for example, will have, in addition to local expenses, apportionments for World Service (global) and conference benevolences (regional). United Methodist funding acknowledges that "we are in this together."

- **Q.:** Are United Methodist liberal or conservative?

  A.: Yes.

- **Q.:** How is power balanced in United Methodism?

  A.: Aware that sin can lead to abuse of power, United Methodist structure disperses authority. For example, the Judicial Council is a judicial branch of the church; the conferences are a legislative branch; the bishops are an executive branch. Each branch has its limits and its roles.

- **Q.:** Are there other questions?

  A.: Yes.

- **Q.:** Are there other answers?

  A.: Not here.

"MORE, MORE!" THE READER EXCITEDLY CRIED

Want to know more (or perhaps forget some of what you learned here)? Here are a few places to continue the journey. Books are available at a Cokesbury store or from www.cokesbury.com.

The official web site of The United Methodist Church is www.umc.org.

The Book of Discipline of The United Methodist Church 2004 (Nashville: United Methodist Publishing House, 2004) [There will be a new edition available after 2008, 2012, 2016, etc.]

NOTES & STUFF